THE FIRST WORLD
WAR
IN PHOTOGRAPHS

THIS IS A SEVENOAKS BOOK

Text copyright © Richard Holmes 2001
Design copyright © Carlton Books Limited 2001

This paperback edition reprinted in 2007 by SevenOaks
An imprint of the Carlton Publishing Group
20 Mortimer Street
London W1T 3 JW

First published in 2001.

A CIP catalogue record for this book is available from the British Library

ISBN 978 1 86200 486 3

Executive Editor Sarah Larter
Art Editor Peter Bailey
Design Simon Mercer and Michelle Campbell
Text and Picture Research Terry Charman and Neil Young
Picture Research Carina Dvorak
Picture co-ordinator Lorna Ainger
Production Garry Lewis and Janette Burgin

Printed in Dubai

IMPERIAL WAR
MUSEUM

THE FIRST WORLD
WAR
IN PHOTOGRAPHS

RICHARD HOLMES

SEVENOAKS

CONTENTS

FOREWORD

I AM VERY PLEASED TO write a foreword to this second collaborative effort between the Imperial War Museum, Carlton Books and Richard Holmes, one of Britain's foremost military historians.

The First World War was the first conflict to be extensively covered by official, press and amateur photographers, and all these have contributed to the museum's photographic archive. Forty-thousand British, Australian and Canadian official photographs formed the basis for the collection, which, since 1918, has grown enormously. Exchanges with former allies and enemies ensured that our First World War collection should be as comprehensive as possible, and these have been augmented over the years by generous donations from members of the public, and by regimental and other associations

From this vast collection Terry Charman and Dr. Neil Young of the museum's Research and Information Department made an initial trawl and Richard Holmes has chosen from their selection the most telling images for inclusion in this book. While some may be familiar to readers, the majority have remained relatively neglected by picture researchers until now. They provide a magnificent pictorial history of what was so rightly called "The Great War".

That the legacy of the First World War remains very much alive to this day was forcibly brought home in June of 2001 by two events. The first was the discovery of a grave containing twenty corpses of men of the 10th Battalion The Lincolnshire Regiment who fell during the Battle of Arras in April 1917; the second the unveiling of a memorial to those men shot for desertion between 1914 and 1918. Both events produced enormous interest in both the media and among the general public. We are compelled yet again to acknowledge how the world we live in today was shaped by the events of the First World War.

I thus commend this book not only to scholars and military historians but to all those interested in what their forebears went through and achieved in "the war that was to end all wars".

Robert Crawford

ROBERT CRAWFORD
Director-General
Imperial War Museum

INTRODUCTION

THE BUILD UP TO WAR

CONTEMPORARIES CALLED IT "the Great War" and it is not hard to see why, for until the greater catastrophe of the Second World War detonated a generation later, the First World War was the largest event of world history. It toppled the "proud tower" of European civilization, which had been built in what was, at least for that continent, the relatively pacific century that followed the end of the Napoleonic wars. It played a key role in transforming old monarchical Europe, helping to sweep away the ruling dynasties in Germany, Russia and Austria-Hungary, and paved the way for political extremism in Germany, Russia and Italy.

Pitched battles and the siege-like progress of trench warfare left broad belts of murdered nature running across both eastern and western Europe and more localized damage elsewhere. There were fierce clashes in Africa, the Levant, and the Middle East, and colonial and naval engagements from the coast of China, through the islands of the Pacific, to the southern oceans and the North Atlantic. It was indeed a world war. Germany and Austria-Hungary, the Central Powers, were joined by Turkey in November 1914 and Bulgaria in October 1915. The Entente of Russia, France and Britain was joined by Japan in August 1914, Italy in May 1915, Portugal in March 1916, Romania that August and Greece in November. China and the nations of South America entered the war on the side of the Entente after the United States joined the conflict in April 1917. Serbia and Belgium were both invaded by the Central Powers in 1914: the former was wholly and the latter largely overrun.

Many of the belligerents had colonies that were themselves caught up in the war, sometimes as scenes of conflict in their own right and more often as sources of manpower for the major fronts. Troops from French colonies in Africa and southeast Asia fought close by men of the British Indian army on the Western Front; Australians and New Zealanders distinguished themselves in Gallipoli and alongside Canadians and South Africans in France; and some Russian troops, in a gesture of inter-Allied solidarity, were sent to fight on the Western Front, which was also home to a large Portuguese contingent.

The war had profound social consequences. Men were swept into the armed forces of the combatant nations on a scale that made light of age and social class: the youngest British soldier killed in the war was the 14-year-old Private John Condon of the Royal Irish Regiment, and the oldest Lieutenant Henry Webber of the South Lancashire Regiment, killed at the age of 68. The daily life of belligerent nations was transformed by the impact of war industry whose insatiable demand for workers was to see, especially in Britain, women assume new roles not only in that arena but also in trades hitherto dominated by men. Civilians were also directly affected by war. Naval blockades strangled inexorably the Central Powers, whose populations suffered from growing shortages of food, and aerial bombardment, still on a tiny scale, gave an ugly foretaste of horrors to come.

It is impossible to quantify the human cost of the war, for the statistics simply do not exist to support accurate calculation, but historians generally agree at a figure of around thirteen million dead. The major combatants lost what were then unprecedented numbers of military dead: 1.2 million for Austria-Hungary, at least 1.7 million for Russia, 1.3 million for France, about 2 million for Germany, a million for Britain and her empire, more than 400,000 for Italy, and 325,000 for Turkey. The US Army lost over 50,000 men in France, most of them killed in fifteen weeks of hard fighting in 1918, and at least one of the reasons for differing attitudes within the Western alliance in the Second World War was the fact that America was not as deeply marked as Britain by the butcher's bill of the previous conflict. The dead were only one element of a burden of casualties, which left at least three times as many men wounded, some hideously crippled in body, others blighted in mind, and still more so bruised by their experiences as to have lost that vital energy which might have driven them to succeed in a variety of professions, not least politics. In more than one sense the Second World War was to prove a legacy of the First.

The literary battle continued long after the war and, although we may suspect that its fiercest clashes are now over, sharp skirmishes still sputter on. This battle of the books was, and to a great extent remains, defined by national viewpoints. One of the many strengths of Hew Strachan's very important book *The First World War: Volume 1: To Arms* (2001) is to describe the conflict as the world war that it demonstrably was. But for many German historians, writing in the aftermath of an even more terrible war, the real issue was the extent to which Germany bore the principal burden of guilt for starting the war, while French historians found it hard to escape the centrality of Verdun and the role of Marshal Philippe Pétain, hero of the 1916 battle but disgraced head of the Second World War Vichy regime. The experience of Gallipoli and the Western Front for long dominated Australian analysis of the war, and the Canadian Corps's achievement on Vimy Ridge in 1917 was so dominant that there is indeed a good case for saying that "Canada became a nation at Vimy." American historians took little interest in the first three years of the war (Barbara Tuchman's wonderful study *August 1914* is an honourable exception), but were more concerned with its political consequences, not simply because of America's importance in the peacemaking process but because of the ongoing debate on her role in the world, for which the 1920s and 1930s provided abundant if ambivalent evidence.

For British historians the debate centred upon the conduct of the war on the Western Front and the relationship between that and other theatres of war. Much of the history and biography written in

the immediate aftermath of the war was relatively uncritical of commanders and politicians, although David Lloyd George's *War Memoirs* took a vicious swipe at the British high command, and there was personal bickering, for instance between the protagonists of Sir John French, replaced as commander in chief of the British Expeditionary Force in December 1915, and those of Sir Douglas Haig, his successor. However, C. R. M. F. Cruttwell's history of the war, first published in 1934, and one of the best of these early works, pointed to "a captious and jealous rigidity of outlook, a purblind psychology" among senior commanders of all nations, and Cruttwell, himself a veteran of the war, paid tribute to the "endurance, patience and good humour so generally shown by the great masses of hastily trained civilians from all the great countries engaged."

It was after the Second World War, however, that this contrast between commanders and the men they led was revealed most sharply, and a school of writers blamed internal factors, most notably the incompetence of senior British commanders, for the worst horrors of the war. Leon Wolff's *In Flanders Fields* (1958) was a savage indictment of the conduct of the Passchendaele campaign of 1917, and Alan Clark's *The Donkeys* (1961) approached the battles of 1915 with the conviction that senior officers were "grossly incompetent for the tasks they had to discharge and that Haig, in particular, was an unhappy combination of ambition, obstinacy and megalomania." Although a few writers like Robert Kee brought freshness and originality to their theme, so much of this was the tragic cliché masquerading as history, with bodies rotting on the barbed wire, rats as big as footballs, and generals who were bluff old incompetents at the best and Machiavellian killers at the worst. The cultural current of the times – for the 1960s were debunking authority more generally – gave added momentum to the criticism. Some books rose above it. Correlli Barnett's *The Swordbearers* (1963) wears its years well, and Alistair Horne's *The Price of Glory* (1962) paints the dreadful Battle of Verdun in colours which the passage of time has not dimmed.

Yet the debunkers did not have it their own way. John Terraine persistently defended the battered reputation of Haig in a series of books, with *Douglas Haig: The Educated Soldier* (1963)

establishing a benchmark in asserting that Haig was right to maintain that "we cannot hope to win until we have defeated the German army" and demonstrating that it was indeed the British army that won the war in its last hundred days in 1918. He emphasized what Keith Simpson has termed external factors, such as "prewar British inexperience and lack of preparation, the problem of adapting to new technology, the fighting power of the German army, restraints imposed by coalition warfare, and political interference." And although Haig was still assailed, most excessively by Denis Winter in *Haig's Command* (1991) and most astutely by Gerard De Groot in *Douglas Haig* (1988), he seems to be emerging from the long battle at least on the winning side, if not actually author of the victory. A growing weight of scholarly opinion now tends to a more balanced view of the war than that of the "Donkeys" school. In his important book *The Killing Ground* (1987) the Canadian historian Tim Travers looked hard at the British view of the nature of war and the personalized structure of its prewar officer corps, and placed Haig in the context of an army that Professor Travers saw as inflexible, preoccupied with the offensive, and convinced that battle was an ordered and methodical activity. The astute John Bourne has rightly observed that this does too little to reflect the very real expertise attained by the British army in 1918. Travers nonetheless broke new ground by going back to primary sources (something conspicuously absent from so much of the Donkeys school) and helping to de-personalize the debate, and his *How the War Was Won* (1992) goes far towards meeting Dr Bourne's criticism of his earlier work. Paddy Griffith's *Battle Tactics of the Western Front: The British Army's Art of Attack 1916-18* (1994) made an important advance by contrasting the fumbling of the early years of the war, itself scarcely surprising given the British army's rapid and unplanned expansion, with its marked tactical improvement after the Somme. There are still astonishing gaps in the literature. Logistics is the subject of only one book, albeit a good one, Ian Malcolm Brown's *British Logistics on the Western Front* (1998); the staff has been the subject of no serious study; major battles like Loos and Cambrai still await proper archive-based analysis; and too much of the English-language work on German command and tactics still stems from too few original sources, though David Zabecki broke new ground with his biography of Ludendorff's artillery expert Georg Bruchmüller (1994). And some issues continue to generate as much heat as light: it would be too much to expect that John Hughes-Wilson's and Cathryn Corns's excellent *Blindfold and Alone* (2001) will close the controversy over the emotive issue of capital courts martial. Despite these shortfalls, a clear path ahead seems to be emerging. Most historians not only balance internal and external factors to get a rounded view of the problem of command but, like Robin Prior and Trevor Wilson in *Command on the Western Front* (1992), combine this with tactical and operational analysis. Many students of the war would agree with Brian Bond and Nigel Cave in *Haig: A Reappraisal Seventy Years On* (1999) that "the British Army's part in the First World War, and Haig's role in particular, should at last be placed in full historical context where there will be less need for emotional partisanship on either side and more dispassionate concern with the complexity of events and the limited scope for the decisive influence of individuals at even the highest level of command."

Yet scholarly analysis of the war is but part of the issue. Most people encounter the war as literature before they read its history, and personal accounts – part memoir and part fiction – like Robert Graves's *Goodbye to All That* (1929) and Siegfried Sassoon's *Memoirs of an Infantry Officer* (1930) were, in their way, as important in shaping attitudes to the war as poets like Sassoon himself, Wilfred Owen and Edward Thomas. The process has continued into our own time, with novels like Pat Barker's *Ghost Road* trilogy and Sebastian Faulks's *Birdsong* enjoying readerships that few historians would dream of and, in the process, popularizing a view of the war which is anything but objective fact. Films, whether overtly ironic like *Oh What a Lovely War* or allegedly serious like *Gallipoli* have generally had the same effect. Much as I love *Blackadder Goes Forth* (and applaud the brave ending of its final episode) there is a danger that that sleek old murderer General Melchett will be taken seriously, and that operations on the Western Front really will be seen as an effort to inch Field Marshal Haig's drinks cabinet ever closer to Berlin.

On the one hand, then, we have historical opinion striving for a genuine understanding of the conflict in all its complex depth. And on the other we have an attitude to the war based on dramatic fiction and a desire, emphasized by the way in which the war is often taught in schools, to empathize with the ordinary man in the mud. In between the two is a gulf between popular understanding and academic scholarship, and one of this book's purposes is to help bridge it. It uses photographs in the Imperial War Museum's collection to do so. These include the work of official war photographers, British, allied and enemy, as well as that of many individuals who used the camera's relatively new-found portability to snap the war. The collection is less comprehensively catalogued than the Museum's Second World War Collections, and there are wider gaps in its coverage: thus while the Russian Revolution is surprisingly well illustrated, military events on the Eastern Front are more patchily recorded. I have tried to avoid the rigged and the posed, and have sometimes challenged long-established captions. One of the benefits of the limited cataloguing, often based on inaccurate contemporary information, has been the surprise discovery of some important but unpublished photographs which had spent the best part of ninety years hidden under a false shadow, as it were.

As was the case with this volume's companion work on the Second World War, this has been very much a team effort, and there were moments when I felt like the worst sort of château general, comfortably working on my plans while Nigel Steel, Terry Charman and Neil Young trudged through the archives at the Museum and Sarah Larter of Carlton Books pounded along the communication trench bearing yet more demands for renewed endeavour. As I look beyond the mud and wire, which seemed to characterize the early stages of the project into the open country revealed by its completion, I am once again reminded, as must be any honest general, that books, like campaigns, are really soldiers' battles.

RICHARD HOLMES

THE PROUD TOWER

The American historian Barbara Tuchman described prewar Europe as "the proud tower", a world which was, for so many of its inhabitants, comfortable, ordered and confident. Much of Europe was ruled by inter-related royal houses, and parliaments were controlled by the affluent middle classes. However, socialist parties grew in strength in response to the discontent of industrial workers with living and working conditions, and in Britain the issues of women's suffrage and Home Rule for Ireland caused substantial ripples on the otherwise placid surface of Edwardian society.

OPPOSITE PAGE
The long hot summer of old England: ladies and gentlemen enjoying themselves at Henley in 1912.

ABOVE
A group of Cambridge students photographed after a May Ball in 1906. Siegfried Sassoon, who was to win a Military Cross, risk court-martial by publicly protesting against the war, and write some of its most moving poetry and prose, is seated on the ground in the centre.

LEFT
The funeral of Britain's King Edward VII in May 1910 united monarchs some of whom would soon be at war. Left to right: Haakon VII of Norway, Ferdinand of Bulgaria, Manoel of Portugal, William II of Germany, George I of Greece, Albert of Belgium. Seated: Alfonso XIII of Spain, George V, Frederick VII of Denmark.

RIGHT

The Entente Cordiale, an Anglo-French rapprochement of 1904, which marked a major shift in British foreign policy, was given impetus by the Francophile Edward VII, seen here on a visit to a visit to Paris in May 1903.

BELOW

There was another side to the social coin: slum accommodation in Britain on the eve of the war.

The German socialist Karl Liebknecht, murdered with Rosa Luxemburg in 1919, addressing a peace demonstration in Berlin in 1911. Although European socialist parties generally opposed war, they were able to exercise little restraining influence in 1914.

To many Britons, the issue of votes for women loomed larger than foreign policy and Ireland loomed larger than both. The funeral of Emily Davison, a militant member of the Women's Social and Political Union, who was killed when she threw herself under the king's horse at the Epsom Derby in 1913 is seen here.

ABOVE
Irish Nationalists demanded Home Rule,
to which many Ulstermen were opposed,
and both sides armed for a clash they
believed inevitable. In 1914 the Irish
parliamentary leader John Redmond
urged the nationalist Irish Volunteers
to support Britain. Those that did so
were called National Volunteers:
here Redmond reviews some of them.

COLONIAL CLASHES

Although there had been no major war in Europe since the Franco-Prussian conflict of 1870–71, there had been clashes elsewhere, some of which gave early indications of the power of modern weapons. In the Anglo-Boer War of 1899–1902 Britain made heavy weather of beating the Boers in South Africa, and the Russo-Japanese War of 1904–5 saw the defeat of Russia by Japan. Closer to home were two Balkan wars, the first (1912–13) resulting in victory by the Balkan Alliance (Bulgaria, Greece, Serbia and Montenegro) over Turkey, and the second (1913) with Bulgaria beaten by Greece, Turkey, Serbia, Montenegro and Romania.

BELOW
When rebellious Boxers, members of a clandestine Chinese patriotic society with strong xenophobic traits, besieged foreign legations at Peking in 1900 an international force was dispatched to relieve them. Here Light F Battery, 5th US Artillery engages Chinese positions on the road to Peking, August 5, 1900. The city was reached nine days later.

LEFT
Japanese infantry outside the Russian fortress and naval base of Port Arthur on the Kwantung peninsula, leased from China in 1898. Blockaded by sea, besieged on land from June 1904, and the target of Japanese heavy guns, Port Arthur eventually surrendered in January 1905. Its long defence suggested that fortresses were anything but obsolete.

BELOW
Trench warfare was not a creation of the First World War. Here British soldiers shelter in a trench at Chieveley on February 4, 1900 during operations to relieve the besieged town of Ladysmith.

Signalmen from a British, German, Austrian and Italian naval landing party during a combined exercise in Albania, circa 1912–13.

Serbian machine gunners at Adrianople during the First Balkan War. Adrianople (now Edirne) was taken from the Turks, but recaptured by them in the Second Balkan war. The belt-fed water-cooled guns are typical of those in use at the period: light machine guns did not emerge until the First World War.

CRISES

Tension between the major European powers grew in the first decade of the twentieth century, with a series of crises, beginning with a Franco-German dispute over Morocco in 1905 and going on to other potential clashes in North Africa and the Balkans. The mood of confrontation encouraged, and was itself fostered by, the constant modernization of weapons and equipment and by an Anglo-German race in warship construction. General Staffs updated plans for general mobilization, whose reliance on early call-up and swift concentration by railway was to give politicians little room for manoeuvre.

ABOVE

Part of Britain's military reform after the Boer War was the creation of a second-line Territorial Force, originally designed for home defence, from the heterogeneous part-time yeomanry, militia and volunteers that had previously constituted the army's volunteer reserves. Here the 1st Westminster Rifles leave Yaverland Camp in July 1909: they wear the 1903 bandolier equipment and carry the long Lee-Enfield rifle.

Kaiser Wilhelm II at the Imperial German army's manoeuvres in 1906. The Kaiser took his military role very seriously, and enjoyed leading the "decisive" cavalry charge at the conclusion of the annual manoeuvres.

The close relationship between British and German ruling houses helped keep Anglo-German relations at least superficially friendly, despite commercial, colonial and naval rivalries. Here Winston Churchill (third from the left, in the uniform of the Queen's Own Oxfordshire Hussars) attends the 1906 Imperial manoeuvres with Lord Lonsdale and other British guests.

ABOVE

A photograph from the collection of
Hugh, 5th Earl of Lonsdale, a personal
friend of the Kaiser, shows Wilhelm's
royal yacht *Hohenzollern* passing through
the newly opened Kiel Canal in June 1895.
The canal enabled warships to move
swiftly from the Baltic to the North Sea,
and caused concern in British naval circles.

RIGHT

Field Marshal Count Alfred von Schlieffen
(1833–1913), Chief of the German General
Staff 1891–1906. Responsible for the plan
which bears his name, Schlieffen planned for
war on two fronts, and proposed to fight
a holding campaign against Russia while
seeking a decisive battle with the French.

RIGHT
The launching in 1906 of HMS *Dreadnought*, the first all-big gun battleship in the world, rendered all other battleships obsolete at a stroke, and signalled a new departure in the Anglo-German naval race.

BELOW
The Royal Navy's 1st and 2nd Battle Squadrons at sea, 1912. Battleships like these were seen as the arbiters of naval warfare, and Britain built them so as to be superior to any two possible adversaries.

1914

NOT OVER BY CHRISTMAS

CHAOS WAS MORE PREVALENT THAN CONSPIRACY IN THE SUMMER OF 1914. THERE WERE CERTAINLY SOME IN GERMANY AND AUSTRIA WHO BELIEVED THAT WAR WAS INEVITABLE AND WISHED FOR IT SOONER RATHER THAN LATER, BEFORE REFORMS INSTITUTED BY RUSSIA AFTER HER DEFEAT IN THE RUSSO-JAPANESE WAR HAD TIME TO TAKE FULL EFFECT. OTHERS, IN FRANCE, FEARED THAT BECAUSE GERMANY'S POPULATION GREW MORE QUICKLY THAN THEIR OWN, THE MANPOWER GAP BETWEEN THEM WOULD WIDEN.

GENERAL STAFFS HAD polished plans for the mobilization of reservists to bring armies up to war strength and for the rapid dispatch of those armies to the frontier by railway: they stressed the danger of allowing an enemy to gain advantage by mobilizing first. There was an air of war-mood across the continent, with popular philosophers and patriotic schoolmasters alike emphasizing the role of war in national identity and a challenge from which only cowards and weaklings would hold back. The loss of Alsace and Lorraine to Germany after the Franco-Prussian War of 1870–1871 still rankled in France, and commercial and colonial rivalry increased friction.

And yet for all this there was nothing pre-ordained about the events of July and August 1914, although they took on an air of inevitability not only to those who lived through them, but also to many of those who have studied them since. The Balkan crisis of July 1914 was undeniably serious, but there had been other serious crises over the past decade. The warmongers were in a minority, and if there were tensions between European states there were also strong links between them. But too many of the major players were dwarfed by the problems they confronted. Worsening communications between potential adversaries and a striking lack of moral courage in high places meant that this time, once the crisis had broken, events spiralled rapidly downwards to take humanity over the lip of the crater.

On June 28, Gavrilo Princip, a young Bosnian Serb, shot the Archduke Franz Ferdinand, heir to the throne of Austria-Hungary, in Sarajevo, capital of the province of Bosnia-Herzegovina, which the Austrians had recently annexed. The Austrians blamed Serbia for supporting Princip and his accomplices, and, confident of support from their ally Germany, presented the Serbs with a sharp ultimatum. When the Serbs rejected it – as they were bound to – Austria duly declared war on them. The Serbs had already appealed to their Slavic brothers in Russia, who began a partial mobilization to deter the Austrians. The Germans warned that they would answer a full Russian mobilization with one of their own: when Russia pressed ahead, Germany duly declared war on August 1. France had refused, on July 31, to guarantee that she would stand aside from the conflict, and Germany declared war on her too on August 3.

Britain's position was ambivalent. The Entente Cordiale was not a formal treaty, and the British government had emphasized that the talks between British and French staffs, in which the dispatch of a British Expeditionary Force (BEF) to France was discussed, were not binding. However, German violation of Belgian neutrality, which had been guaranteed by a treaty to which Britain was a signatory, made it difficult for her to stand aside. In any event the Foreign Secretary, Sir Edward Grey, pointed out that a German victory would be inimical to British interests, and when Germany declined to withdraw from Belgium, Britain declared war on her on August 4.

The German war plan had been devised by General Alfred von Schlieffen, who feared that Germany could win only "ordinary victories" against the Russians, who would withdraw into their vast empire. France, in contrast, could be beaten decisively. Schlieffen, fascinated by Hannibal's defeat of the Romans at Cannae in 216 BC, planned an enveloping attack in which the armies of the German right wing would swing through Belgium, hooking round Paris to catch the French in a battle of encirclement. If the French launched their own offensive to recover Alsace and Lorraine they would do the Germans "a kindly favour" by pushing deeper into the trap. A small force would be left to mask the Russians, who would be beaten and forced to sue for peace when German armies turned eastwards after victory in France.

Schlieffen had reservations about the plan, fearing that the Germans were simply not strong enough, and his successor, General Helmuth von Moltke (known as "the younger" to distinguish him from his uncle, the architect of German victory in 1870–71) made changes that weakened the all-important right wing. But it was to come close to success, not least because the French, in a brusque rejection of the defensive-mindedness, which had cost them so dear in 1870, were to launch "Plan 17", an all-out offensive into the lost provinces, in an effort to impose Gallic *élan*, in white gloves and red trousers, on German field-grey and machine guns.

Mobilization and concentration went much as intended, with enormous patriotic enthusiasm in Europe's great cities veiling a myriad of private griefs as so many reservists recognized that what one called "the tear season" had begun. In the west, the German advance through Belgium was delayed by the gallant Belgian defence of Liège, the last of whose forts fell on August 16. However, although the French offensive – "the Battle of the Frontiers" – began promisingly, between August 20 and 24, it was bloodily repulsed in a dreadful demonstration of the effect of firepower on bodies of brave men. Moltke ill-advisedly permitted the local commander, Crown Prince Rupprecht of Bavaria, to counterattack.

The French were also in trouble in the north, where their left-hand army, Lanrezac's Fifth, was beaten at Charleroi. Field Marshal Sir John French's BEF, at 120,000 men a mere frigate among the battleships of continental war, was on Lanrezac's left, and on August 23, it fought a sharp battle at Mons before falling back to conform with Lanrezac's retreat. Its two corps were divided by the Forest of Mormal, and on August 26, II Corps administered a "stopping blow" at Le Cateau, at the cost of almost 8,000 men and 39 guns.

The retreat took the allies back to the Marne east of Paris where the summer's campaign reached its culmination. Schlieffen had emphasized that the outermost German army, Kluck's First, was to swing west of Paris, but a combination of crises at the front and lack of firm directing will from Moltke saw it edge eastwards, offering a flank that was attacked by the Paris garrison and Manoury's newly formed Sixth Army. The blow was not decisive, for Kluck was able to turn to meet it, but in doing so he opened up a gap between his army and the Second. The British, despite the entreaties of General Joseph Joffre, the French commander-in-chief, were slow to exploit this, but Fifth Army, under a new commander, fought hard, and the new Ninth Army, under General Ferdinand Foch, who had made his reputation as a corps commander at Nancy, also attacked vigorously. The German failure was as much moral as material. Lieutenant Colonel Hentsch, a staff officer sent down by Moltke, authorized the armies of the right wing to fall back. However, the first month of the war had done terrible damage to the French army, which lost 212,000 men, about twenty per cent of its mobilized strength and nearly forty per cent of its regular officers.

Many contemporaries thought that the Marne was a decisive battle in the old sense, and that the Germans would retreat to their frontiers and sue for peace. But on September 9–13 they fell back on to the River Aisne, where the British attacked them in a hopeless battle that saw Sir John French admit that they had entered a new sort of war in which "the *spade* will be as great a necessity as the rifle, and the heaviest types and calibres of artillery will be brought up on either side." With the defence lines solidified to the southeast, in September and October the adversaries pushed northwards, each seeking to outflank the other, in "the race to the sea", which was to end with a continuous front running from the Swiss border to the Flanders coast.

In the process the BEF was moved north, and mid-October found it around the little Belgian town of Ypres, first attacking in the belief that it had found the German flank, and then defending as the Germans threw their own weight into the sector. A small British force had been sent to Antwerp in an unavailing attempt to help the Belgians defend it. Part of the force escaped capture when the city fell, and moved south to join the BEF at Ypres. The First Battle of Ypres ground into the winter, with crises on October 31 and November 11, and although the BEF held Ypres it paid a heavy price for the privilege, losing over 58,000 officers and men.

As trench lines hardened in the west, the war in the east was far more mobile. The Russians responded to French appeals for prompt assistance by advancing into East Prussia, with General Pavel Rennenkampf's First Army beating the Prussian Eighth Army at Gumbinnen on August 20, while, 160 kilometres (100 miles) to the southwest, Samsonov's Second Army made good progress against weak opposition. The dispirited German commander was replaced by General Paul von Hindenburg, recalled from retirement, with Major General Erich Ludendorff as his chief of staff. The pair – the stern, imperturbable and patrician Hindenburg and the overbearing, energetic and middle-class Ludendorff – were a formidable combination, and built on a plan devised by the army's head of operations, Colonel Max Hoffmann, to destroy the Russian armies separately. Aided by wireless intercepts and the comprehensive railway network, they first concentrated against Samsonov, smashing him at Tannenberg in late August, and then went on to beat Rennenkampf in September around the Masurian Lakes and drive deep into Poland. These victories lacerated the trained manpower of an army that had made considerable improvements since the Russo-Japanese war, and the part they played in the eventual collapse of tsarism cannot be underestimated.

The fact that the Russian army was anything but a moribund juggernaut was proved further south, where the Austrians mounted an ambitious attack from northeast Galicia, aimed at the flank of the Russian concentration east of Warsaw. However, General Alexei Alexeivich Brusilov, commanding the Russian Eighth Army, bundled back the Austrian left flank, eventually overrunning the Bukovina. Although the balance was more finely weighted further north around Lemberg (modern Lvov), by mid-September the Russians had roundly beaten the Austrians, driving them back behind the River San, taking the fortress of Jaroslav and blockading Przemysl.

An Austrian punitive expedition invaded northwest Serbia in August and was heavily defeated. A far bigger offensive was launched in early November, and though the Austrians took the Serbian capital Belgrade they were even more badly beaten in early December, losing 40,000 prisoners. The Austro-Hungarian army, whose heterogeneous composition was evidence of the wide racial and linguistic mix that characterized the empire itself, was scarcely less damaged by these early defeats than were the Russians by their misfortunes in East Prussia and Poland.

The balance of naval power favoured the Entente, for the Royal Navy alone was significantly superior to the navies of Germany and Austria: only in the number and quality of submarines did the Germans have an advantage. On the initiative of Winston Churchill, First Lord of the Admiralty, the fleet did not disperse after a trial mobilization in July 1914, and when war broke out it was deployed to face Germany, with the bulk of the Grand Fleet at Scapa Flow in the Orkneys. The methodical Admiral Sir John Jellicoe assumed command, and carried out several sweeps in the North Sea in the hope of finding his enemy, the German High Seas Fleet, though this remained resolutely in harbour. There were naval actions elsewhere, most notably in the southern oceans, where Admiral von Spee's China Squadron sank HMS *Good Hope* and HMS *Monmouth* off Coronel but was itself all but annihilated off the Falklands on December 8.

The popular enthusiasm of August 1914 anticipated a short war, with men "home before the leaves fall." Many professional soldiers, however, feared that the combination of armed alliances, modern firepower and large, determined armies would produce a protracted conflict. Schlieffen himself had warned that only a quick victory could prevent stalemate. And as autumn hardened into winter, the war showed no sign of ending but was already taking on the characteristics of an enormous siege.

THE OUTBREAK OF WAR

The assassination of the Archduke Franz Ferdinand, heir to the throne of Austria-Hungary, in Sarajevo, capital of the Austrian province of Bosnia-Herzegovina, precipitated a crisis that led to war. The armies of Europe's great powers were brought up to strength by the mobilization of reservists, and clattered off to concentration areas on the frontiers on trains whose methodical departure gave rise to the phrase "war by timetable." The French were to say that men were "eaten by the Gare de l'Est" and many of the young men who entered the maws of the great metropolitan termini that summer were never to return.

ABOVE
On June 28, Franz Ferdinand and his wife Sophie descend the steps of Sarajevo's town hall into the car which will take them, minutes later, to death under Gavrilo Princip's bullets.

RIGHT
Gavrilo Princip (1894–1918) was a member of the Black Hand secret society, dedicated to freeing southern Slav peoples from Austrian rule. A mistake by their chauffeur gave him an unexpected opportunity to shoot the royal couple at close range with his pistol. Princip, too young for the death penalty, died of tuberculosis in an Austrian prison.

ABOVE
Austrian soldiers wave cheerfully
as they depart for war. In fact, the
Austro-Hungarian army was a rich mix
of nationalities, not all of whom greeted
the outbreak of war with such glee.

ABOVE
German reservists, still in civilian clothes,
depart in a train whose graffiti vividly
depicts popular enthusiasm for a war
seen as being short and victorious.

LEFT

A crowd in Munich celebrates the declaration of war. The inset shows the young Adolf Hitler who volunteered for war service in a Bavarian infantry regiment.

OVERLEAF

A woman marching alongside French troops as they leave for the front, August 1914.

BELOW

French reservists leaving the Gare du Nord in Paris on their way to their regimental depots, where they will receive uniforms and equipment.

The Russian army was in the process of reform following its defeat in the Russo-Japanese war, and although much better than is often suggested it lacked the industrial power-base to sustain a long attritional war.

Crowds outside Buckingham Palace on the evening of August 3, where the King, Queen and Prince of Wales appeared on the balcony at 9 p.m. to rapturous applause. Mobilization had already been declared, though there would not be a formal state of war between Britain and Germany for another 26 hours.

ABOVE

Reservists of the Grenadier Guards
reporting for duty, August 5–6. About half
the soldiers who went to France with
the BEF in 1914 were regular reservists,
recalled to the colours on the outbreak of
war. Volunteer members of the Territorial
Force were not liable for service overseas,
but many immediately volunteered for it.

THE ESCAPE OF THE GOEBEN

There was a small German squadron in the Mediterranean, the powerful battle cruiser *Goeben* and the light cruiser *Breslau*. The British had a large squadron under Admiral Sir Berkeley Milne and a smaller one of four armoured cruisers, four light cruisers and sixteen destroyers under Rear Admiral Troubridge. Troubridge, over-emphasizing his instructions not to engage a superior force, did not bring *Goeben* to battle, fearing that her superior firepower could have destroyed his squadron piecemeal. The Germans reached Constantinople unmolested, and their arrival in what was still a neutral port had considerable impact on bringing Turkey into the war on Germany's side in October.

BELOW
The battle cruiser *Goeben*, flagship of Rear Admiral Souchon's German Mediterranean squadron, at Genoa on May 7, 1914.

FIRST SHOTS

Expeditions were mounted against Germany's overseas colonies as soon as war broke out. Their initial aim was to deprive Germany of naval bases in which detached squadrons or individual commerce-raiders might shelter and refuel, but the capture of German colonies was soon seen as the acquisition of bargaining chips in case of a compromise peace.

ABOVE
Australian and New Zealand troops mounted expeditions against Samoa and isolated German possessions in the Pacific. Here we see New Zealanders in Samoa in August.

RIGHT
Lieutenant George Masterman Thompson of the Royal Scots was the first British officer to be killed in the war. He died on August 22, while commanding a small force of Senegalese troops at Chra in German Togoland.

THE WAR AT SEA

Although 1914 did not bring the decisive naval battle expected by many, there were several smaller actions. In August a British incursion into the Heligoland Bight drew German pursuers within range of a squadron of lurking battle cruisers, and four German light cruisers were lost. A British squadron was all but destroyed off Coronel on November 1 but the victorious German squadron was beaten shortly afterwards. The commerce-raider *Emden* wreaked havoc in the Indian Ocean before falling victim to HMAS *Sydney* in November. Most portentously, one German submarine sank three British armoured cruisers in a single engagement.

LEFT

Death of a minelayer. On August 4–5, the German minelayer *Königin Luise* laid mines in the Thames estuary but was sunk on her way home, the first vessel lost in the war. Shortly afterwards the light cruiser HMS *Amphion* was lost on one of her mines.

BELOW

The armoured cruiser HMS *Aboukir*. On September 22 the elderly armoured cruisers HMS *Aboukir*, HMS *Cressy* and HMS *Hogue* were patrolling off the Dutch coast with no easily discernible purpose when they were torpedoed in turn by Commander Weddigern of U-9 with the loss of 1,459 lives.

On the afternoon of August 28, as the mist gathered, Vice-Admiral Beatty's battle cruisers arrived at speed to support British destroyers that had penetrated the Heligoland Bight and were being pursued by German light cruisers. This photograph apparently shows the destruction of one of the German vessels.

Rear Admiral Cradock flew his flag in the armoured cruiser HMS *Good Hope*. On November 1, in company with HMS *Monmouth* and HMS *Glasgow*, with the old battleship HMS *Canopus* well astern, he fought the China Squadron off Coronel. *Good Hope* and *Monmouth* were lost with all hands, among them these officers of *Good Hope*, photographed at the Falklands on October 18.

ABOVE
Admiral von Spee's victorious
China Squadron, with the armoured
cruisers *Scharnhorst* and *Gneisenau*,
and the light cruisers *Leipzig*, *Nürnberg*
and *Dresden* in line ahead off the
coast of Chile, November 16–29.

ABOVE

Spee reached the Falklands but found that
Vice Admiral Sturdee's more powerful battle
cruisers were already there. Only *Dresden*
escaped. *Gneisenau* fought for nearly five
hours, and her crew formed up to give three
cheers for the Kaiser as she sank. Spee and
his two sons died in the battle. Here, HMS
Inflexible picks up survivors.

ABOVE

On November 9, the commerce-raider *Emden* was caught at Cocos Island by HMAS *Sydney* and beached after a hard-fought battle: here we see her on the rocks at North Keeling. Captain Müller had behaved with punctilious legality throughout his cruise, and he and his officers were allowed to retain their swords.

THE BEF IN FRANCE

Sir John French's BEF, initially a cavalry division and four infantry divisions, with another division arriving in late August, crossed safely to France and concentrated around Maubeuge. It advanced northwards to conform to the French plan, fighting its first battle at Mons on August 23 and then falling back. Three days later II Corps under General Sir Horace Smith-Dorrien paused at Le Cateau to rebuff the pursuing Germans, and the BEF continued its retreat to the Marne. It then advanced to the Aisne where it launched fruitless attacks on Germans well dug in on the wooded spurs overlooking the river.

ABOVE

Field Marshal Sir John French lands at Boulogne from HMS *Sentinel* on August 14, with the French military attaché Colonel Huguet behind him. A brave man of great personal warmth, French was the most distinguished cavalry officer of his generation, but proved out of his depth in large-scale continental war.

BELOW

Highlanders arriving in Boulogne. Most of the BEF landed at Le Havre and Cherbourg before proceeding by rail to its concentration area.

Private Carter of D Company,
4th Battalion The Middlesex Regiment
on guard in Obourg, just east of Mons,
on August 22. His battalion was
heavily engaged there the following day.

Men of 4th Battalion The Royal Fusiliers in
the main square at Mons on August 22. The
next day this battalion held the Mons-Condé
canal at Nimy, just north of Mons, where
Lieutenant Dease and Private Godley won
the first two Victoria Crosses of the war.

ABOVE
Lieutenant Colonel P. R. Robertson
(centre), commanding 1st Battalion The
Cameronians (Scottish Rifles) confers
with his mounted adjutant and a company
commander at Le Cateau, August 26.

OPPOSITE
Captain the Hon. C. Mulholland,
11th Hussars, snatches a rest in
the Forest of Ermenouville
during the retreat to the Marne.

RIGHT

On the foggy morning of September 1 a British cavalry brigade was caught off-guard at Néry, where its horse artillery battery was wiped out. The British counterattack drove the Germans back: here we see men of the 2nd Dragoon Guards (Queen's Bays) with prisoners.

BELOW

British units had French officers and NCOs attached to them for liaison and interpreting duties: the French Impressionist painter Paul Maze spent the war with the Royal Scots Greys. This shot shows British and French soldiers outside a café in August or early September.

OPPOSITE

The advance to the Aisne: 1st Cameronians on the march near La Haute Maison, September 6. Long straight roads lined with poplar trees were a feature of the infantryman's life that blazing summer.

BELGIUM

Belgium was neutral, and planned to defend her borders
before withdrawing on the "national redoubt" at Antwerp.
Fortifications there, and at Namur and Liège, embodied
armoured steel cupolas developed by the engineer Brialmont.
Liège, blocking the gap between the "Maastricht appendix"
of Dutch territory and the hilly Ardennes, halted the German
advance, but its forts proved no match for German heavy guns
which methodically smashed them. The Belgian field army withdrew
westwards to Antwerp, attacked by the Germans in late September.
Despite British support, Antwerp proved untenable, though part
of the Belgian army escaped to hold the line on the River Yser.

BELOW
German soldiers pose on top of a cupola
at Fort Loncin, one of the Liège forts,
knocked out by a German siege howitzer.

ABOVE
Genuine combat shots are comparatively
rare: this one shows Belgian troops
defending a hasty roadblock in the town of
Alost. The position was forced shortly after
the photographer, Frank Brockliss, departed.

RIGHT
Belgian *Carabiniers*, in their distinctive hats,
during the retreat to Antwerp on August 20.
Their machine guns are drawn by dogs.

ABOVE

Refugees fleeing to Holland
from bombarded Antwerp.

THE EASTERN FRONT

In accordance with Schlieffen's principles, the Germans entrusted the defence of East Prussia to a single army, Prittwitz's Eighth. When Prittwitz panicked in the face of an unexpectedly rapid Russian advance he was replaced by Hindenburg and Ludendorff. They first beat the Russian First and Second Armies at Tannenberg and the Masurian Lakes and then drove deep into Poland. On the southern part of the Eastern Front, however, Germany's Austrian Allies were roughly handled by a Russian counteroffensive.

ABOVE
Hindenburg (centre in light greatcoat) and his staff just before the Battle of Tannenberg. Ludendorff, hands in pockets, stands on his right, and Colonel Max Hoffmann, who conceived the plan for the battle, is on his left.

ABOVE
Tsar Nicholas II (left) with his uncle Grand Duke Nicholas Nicholaievich. An experienced professional, Nicholas was appointed commander in chief on August 1. When the Tsar assumed personal command in mid-1915 the Grand Duke was sent to the Caucasus front, and captured Armenia from the Turks.

LEFT
Russian prisoners in Poland
in the autumn of 1914.

BELOW
The Eastern Front was about twice as long
as the Western, and its sheer scale helped
keep operations more fluid even after the
Western Front had locked into stalemate.
Austrian cavalry on the plains in late 1914.

ABOVE
Like their German allies, the
Austrians had some good heavy guns:
here they assemble a 30.5-cm howitzer.

THE WESTERN FRONT

After the front solidified on the Aisne both sides sought to turn their enemy's flank by advancing northwards in "the race to the sea". The BEF was pulled out of the line on the Aisne and shifted to the northern sector around Ypres, where it fought the First Battle of Ypres in October and November. Ypres, the only moderate-sized Belgian town still in Allied hands, had enormous psychological importance, and was retained by the British throughout the war.

BELOW
A British infantry battalion marching into Ypres, October 14, 1914.

A British 18-pdr field gun, the mainstay of
the Royal Field Artillery, in a camouflaged
position south of Ypres, October 19–20.

There was heavy fighting around
Armentières, south of Ypres, in
October. Here men of 1st Cameronians
travel by London buses from
Vlamertinghe to Laventie, on their
way to the trenches, October 19.

ABOVE

A Gurkha unit marches down a muddy
lane shortly after arriving near Rouen.
Indian troops arrived in France in
October 1914, and in December the
Indian Corps became operational.
It remained in France for a year, during
which time it lost 32,727 officers and men.

BELOW

Survivors of the London Scottish, the first
Territorial battalion to go into action.
Wearing kilts of distinctive "hodden grey",
its men attacked on Messines Ridge, just
south of Ypres, on October 31, and 321
out of 750 were hit; thereafter, there were
fewer jokes about "Saturday night soldiers".

Captain Moorhouse of 2nd Argyll and
Sutherland Highlanders sniping in the Bois
Grenier sector, south of Ypres, November.

Digging out a trench below Aubers Ridge
in November. These early trenches were
primitive by comparison with later defences,
and in sectors like this, where the water
table was high – note the pollarded willows
characteristic of this boggy ground –
they were always at risk of flooding.

ABOVE

The Royal Dublin Fusiliers' trenches
at St Yvon in December. The large jar in
the foreground held the rum ration.
It bore the letters "SRD", which
officially stood for Supply Reserve
Depot, but were widely believed
to mean Seldom Reaches Destination.

RIGHT

Ypres owed its importance to the
cloth trade, and its crowning glory
was the huge covered market known
as the Cloth Hall, begun in the thirteenth
century. Here we see it after the
first German bombardment of the
town on November 22; it was
subsequently reduced to rubble.

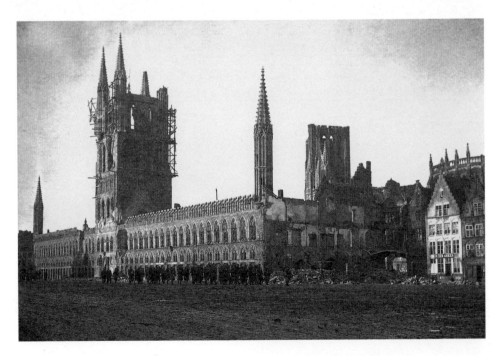

ANTWERP

The Belgian field army of around 65,000 men fell back on the
"national redoubt" of Antwerp. Although the attacking force was
too small to invest the city, powerful German guns outclassed those
in the forts, and the outer defences were penetrated on October 1.
The Allies promised reinforcements, and Churchill encouraged King
Albert to delay the departure of his army. The British sent a naval
division with a marine brigade composed largely of pensioners
and two brigades of woefully inexperienced naval reservists.
More substantial reinforcements failed to arrive in time. The city
capitulated on October 9, but many of its defenders escaped.

ABOVE
Royal Marine pensioners, recalled
to service and wearing the Brodrick cap,
introduced in 1905, avail themselves of
rations supplied by local well-wishers.

ABOVE

The last train out of Antwerp, packed with
men of the 2nd Naval Brigade. The British
lost about 1000 captured and 1,500
driven to internment in nearby Holland.

COLONIAL OPERATIONS

The Allies began an immediate attack on Germany's colonies, most of which were speedily overrun. Japan entered the war on the Allied side on August 23, and at once attacked the strongly fortified German base of Tsingtao on the coast of China.

ABOVE
Men of the South Wales Borderers landing at Tsingtao after its capture by the Japanese.

RIGHT
German naval officers and ratings captured at Tsingtao in a prisoner-of-war camp in Japan. In contrast to her behaviour in the Second World War, Japan's treatment of prisoners of war was impeccable in the First World War.

THE WAR IN THE AIR

On the outbreak of war all major powers had some form of air force, with heavier- and lighter-than-air machines. Air forces were still firmly linked to existing armed services: in Britain the centralized Royal Flying Corps (RFC) split in 1914, leaving the RFC attached to the army and the Royal Naval Air Service (RNAS) to the navy.

ABOVE
Commander Samson's Eastchurch Squadron of the RNAS at Dunkirk early in the campaign. The aircraft are, left to right, a Short 42, a Sopwith tractor, a BE2A and a Henri Farman F20, with an airship in the background.

AEROPLANES ON PARADE
FOR

LORD ROBERTS'S INSPECTION
NETHERAVON. 29/6/14.

ABOVE

Aircraft at the Central Flying School, then at Netheravon on Salisbury Plain, await inspection by Lord Roberts, June 29, 1914. Some pilots wore RFC uniform, which included a characteristic double-breasted tunic, while others, attached to the corps from their own units, dressed regimentally.

THE GERMAN ARMY IN THE WEST

Although the Germans' invasion plan did not work as its
authors hoped, it took them to within measurable distance
of success. And even after the front solidified across France in
the autumn of 1914 the Germans were in a strong position.
The line bulged southwestwards at Noyon, only 96 kilometres
(60 miles) from Paris, and some of France's richest industrial areas,
including the mines of Lille and Douai, lay behind the German lines.

BELOW
German reinforcements on their
way to the front in the autumn of
1914 with a column of ambulances
moving in the opposite direction.

OPPOSITE
A German trench, Flanders 1914. Having
wet feet for a long period could cause trench
foot, a condition akin to frostbite. Men
were encouraged to change socks as often as
possible, easier said than done, and to rub
preparations like whale oil into their feet.

OVERLEAF
A German snowman, equipped with spiked
helmet and Mauser 98 rifle, winter 1914.

THE FRENCH ARMY

Most European armies shared the conviction that only resolute
moral qualities would enable men to achieve results on a densely
held battlefield dominated by the breech-loading rifle and the
machine gun. The French army elevated moral superiority to a cult,
and began the war with a determined offensive which failed in the
face of German firepower. That it survived the first few weeks of
the war, inches from defeat, speaks much for the robust resilience
of Joffre, its commander in chief, who sacked the incompetent
and the unlucky and kept his battered citizen army at its task.

RIGHT

General Joseph Joffre, whose benign
exterior gave him the nickname "Papa",
flanked by his very competent deputy
Castelnau (left) and Pau (right) who
had lost his left hand in the Franco-Prussian
War and was recalled from retirement
to command the Army of Alsace.

LEFT

The 21st Infantry Regiment marching
through the streets of Rouen, August
1914. French infantry went to war in
blue greatcoats, buttoned back to free the
legs for marching, and red trousers. Their
rifle, the 8-mm Lebel, was fitted with a long
cruciform bayonet nicknamed "Rosalie".

Dismounted dragoons, their brass helmets protected by cotton covers, man Hotchkiss machine guns in the Argonne.

The French raised *Spahis*, native light cavalry, in Tunisia, Morocco and Algeria. These fine natural soldiers were armed with sabre and carbine and rode tough little Barb stallions with traditional North African saddlery.

ABOVE
The infantryman was a beast of burden.
These tired and heavily laden men are
coming out of the line in the Argonne.

THE NEW ARMY

Field Marshal Lord Kitchener, the towering military figure
of his generation, was appointed Secretary of State for War in
August. He gained parliamentary approval to raise 500,000 men,
and at once appealed for the first 100,000 volunteers: he had
obtained a staggering 761,000 in the first eight weeks of the war.
These "New Armies" were raised through the adjutant general's
branch at the War Office, and the influx of recruits collapsed the
existing mechanism for enlisting and training. Much of this
manpower was of high quality, but lack of all sorts of resources
made it hard to turn willing volunteers into trained soldiers.

BELOW
The Central London Recruiting Office
off Whitehall in August. Recruiting peaked
on September 3, when 33,204 men were
enlisted, nationwide, in a single day.

ABOVE

A potential recruit takes the eyesight test. The recruiting apparatus was designed to accept an annual intake of 30,000 men, and hard-pressed medical officers and civilian doctors often passed recruits with poor vision and other defects.

RIGHT

Recruits, holding the Bible, take the oath to defend "His Majesty, his heirs and successors, in person, crown and dignity against all enemies …" These lads have dressed up for the occasion, and the fact that the attesting officer is standing with the aid of a crutch suggests that he is a regular, wounded in the war's opening battles.

PREVIOUS PAGES
Most Kitchener recruits joined "service" battalions of country regiments: these often had an unofficial title as well as a formal one: thus 11th Battalion the East Lancashire Regiment lives in history as the Accrington Pals. These recruits to the Lincolnshire Regiment may belong to its 10th Battalion, the Grimsby Chums.

BELOW
There were too few khaki uniforms for all new recruits, and many, like these volunteers of the Royal Field Artillery in training at Mytchett in Hampshire, wore "Kitchener Blue". Its resemblance to postman's uniform made it bitterly unpopular, and the issue of khaki was an important status marker.

THE BOMBARDMENT OF BRITAIN

German cruisers, crossing the North Sea under cover of darkness, launched occasional attacks on British coastal towns. On November 3, Yarmouth and Lowestoft were bombarded, and on December 16, Hartlepool, Whitby and Scarborough were hit. Although civilian casualties were relatively light, the fact that they included woman and children caused great resentment, and the bombardment strengthened popular resolve.

ABOVE
The coffin of Postman Beale, killed on duty at Scarborough, is escorted to the grave by the town's postmen.

PRISONERS OF WAR

On the outbreak of war belligerents interned enemy aliens living
on their territory, and the first clashes saw both sides capture
substantial numbers of prisoners who were housed in
extemporized camps which soon grew in size and permanency.

ABOVE
British civilians interned in Ruhleben
Camp, Berlin. Before its conversion
to a camp, Ruhleben, like Newbury,
opposite, was a race course.

ABOVE
German prisoner-of-war quarters in stables
at Newbury Race Course, October 1914.

THE CHRISTMAS TRUCE

At Christmas 1914 there were a number of unofficial truces on both the Western and Eastern fronts. In France and Belgium officers and men simply met and chatted in No Man's Land, and there were some cases of football being played, apparently not in a formal game but "just a general kickabout." Many combatants would have agreed with Private William Tapp of the Warwicks that "it doesn't seem right to be killing each other at Xmas time."

ABOVE
Officers and men of the Northumberland Hussars in the Armentières sector meet Germans on No Man's Land during a truce in which the dead of earlier attacks were buried.

RIGHT
Second Lieutenant Cyril Drummond, Royal Field Artillery, took this photograph of British and Germans on Boxing Day. "They were very nice fellows to look at," he recalled, "and one of them said 'we don't want to kill you and you don't want to kill us. So why shoot?'."

1915

THE WAR SETS HARD

THE YEAR BEGAN WITH A DEBATE THAT WAS TO DOMINATE BRITISH STRATEGY: KITCHENER TOLD SIR JOHN FRENCH THAT "FEELING HERE IS GAINING GROUND THAT, ALTHOUGH IT IS ESSENTIAL TO DEFEND THE LINE WE NOW HOLD, TROOPS OVER AND ABOVE WHAT IS NECESSARY FOR THAT SERVICE COULD BE BETTER EMPLOYED ELSEWHERE."

FRENCH HAD ALREADY agreed with Joffre that he would take over more of the line and collaborate in a two-pronged offensive against the great salient that jutted out towards Noyon, with an Anglo-French attack in the north and a French offensive in the south. He also had plans for an attack of his own along the Flanders coast. Sending troops away from France would, he warned Kitchener, "simply play the German game," for the war could only be won by beating the German army. This was to be the mainstay of the westerners' position, while the easterners were to argue that there were more promising theatres elsewhere, where the attacker would not inevitably confront the hardening crust of defence.

The question had profound implications for what was, from start to finish, an alliance war. On the one hand the French were unlikely to applaud any plan which did not offer the prospect of getting the Germans off French soil, and this helped shackle Britain to an offensive strategy based on concentration in France. On the other, allies elsewhere were to demand help without which they might collapse, enabling the Germans to throw extra weight on to the Western Front.

A Russian appeal for assistance was the genesis of the Dardanelles expedition, although ironically the Russians proved victorious in the Caucasus at the very time that the British and French decided to act in their support. The Allies proposed to force the passage of the narrow Dardanelles and then cross the Sea of Marmara to threaten Constantinople. They hoped to do this by naval action alone, and the Admiralty had numerous obsolete but heavily armed warships which seemed ideal for the task. The outer forts were silenced easily, but while these operations were in progress, the British

and French governments decided that they could spare troops for an expedition, though it was not certain whether it would be best to use them to reinforce the attack on the Dardanelles by landing on the Gallipoli peninsula, or to support the Serbs. However, although the Greeks were prepared to assist in the latter project, the Russians vetoed it.

On March 18, the Allied fleet attempted to force the Narrows, only to desist when four capital ships, one French and three British, struck mines. The fleet's British commander, Admiral de Robeck, told General Sir Ian Hamilton, commanding the expeditionary force, based at Mudros on the island of Lemnos, that he could not get through without the army's help. The Turks, meanwhile, placed their troops in the area under the command of the German general Liman von Sanders, and when the Allies landed on April 25, they had mixed fortunes. The Australian and New Zealand Army Corps (ANZAC) landed without opposition on the west coast of the peninsula, and might have reached the central peak of Chunuk Bair had it not been for the intervention of Lieutenant Colonel Mustapha Kemal, the future Kemal Atatürk. Further south, around Cape Helles, some beaches were taken without a fight, but at Sedd-el-Bahr (V Beach) the attackers met point-blank fire and got ashore only with enormous difficulty.

Although these handholds were secured over the days that followed, it proved impossible for either side to break the stalemate. Heavily reinforced, on August 6, Hamilton tried again, making a fresh landing at Suvla Bay, while the Australians and New Zealanders mounted an attack north of Anzac Cove. The Turks narrowly held their own at Anzac, while at Suvla pitifully weak command allowed an overwhelming force to build up on the beach, and when it eventually advanced, across a plain dominated by Turkish-held heights, it was cut to pieces. With this tragic failure the campaign had exhausted both military potential and political capital. The French now favoured switching troops to Salonika, where Sarrail, one of their few hotly republican generals, was appointed to the command. Suvla and Anzac were evacuated by December 20, and troops were withdrawn from Helles by January 9. The evacuation was so skilfully handled that its news was received in the Allied capitals almost like that of a victory.

The causes of the costly fiasco at Gallipoli lay as much in strategic uncertainty as failure by commanders on the ground. The campaign was allocated only limited resources, and Hamilton, who would have been a greater general had he not been so nice a man, was as reluctant to press for more as he was to cudgel some of his subordinates. He might have won a decisive victory had he been reinforced sooner, and the fact that he was not testified to Allied preoccupation with the Western Front. This was not unreasonable. What was unreasonable was a failure to link the two campaigns so that priorities were clearly established and conflicting demands reconciled. And for this the lack of an effective high-level command structure, personal and political ambition, and a lack of intellectual rigour alike are to blame.

Sir John French hoped to launch an offensive along the Flanders coast, but the lack of naval support, in view of commitments made to the Dardanelles, combined with French opposition to rule it out. He remained committed to providing part of the northern tine of Joffre's two-pronged offensive, but Joffre cancelled the scheme when the British announced that the 29th Division, the last all-regular formation, was to be sent to the Dardanelles rather than France. The BEF attacked on its own, and at Neuve Chapelle on March 10, General Sir Douglas Haig's First Army assaulted behind a short but intense bombardment and came very close to breaking the German line. The Germans recognized that a few isolated machine guns behind their shattered front had proved invaluable, and learned their lesson well, beginning the construction of an entire second position behind their first, screened from it, where possible, by rising ground,

and far enough back to make an attacker who took the first position move his field guns before he could engage the second.

In the meantime Joffre had mounted two unsuccessful local attacks, one in eastern Champagne and the other at St Mihiel, south of Verdun, before he revived his projected two-pronged attack. The Germans struck first: on April 22, they attacked the junction of the French with the British Second Army at Ypres behind a wave of poison gas. They were ill-prepared to capitalize on their success, and the British counterattacked energetically, but to little purpose and at great cost. Sir Horace Smith-Dorrien of Second Army, who had never got on with Sir John French, was sent home and replaced by General Sir Herbert Plumer, who pulled back to a line closer to Ypres, where the front stabilized for the next two years. The Second Battle of Ypres overshadowed the British contribution to the French offensive, with failed attacks first at Aubers Ridge and then at Festubert, in May. The French attacks went scarcely better, although in Artois, where the French hoped to seize the dominant Vimy Ridge, a corps commanded by General Philippe Pétain, a big, wintry officer who had been on the eve of retirement when war broke out, made a remarkable advance, which was too isolated to have real significance but marked Pétain out for greater things.

H. H. Asquith's Liberal government, in growing difficulties over its conduct of the war, partly because of the "shells scandal" whipped up by newspaper reports on the paucity of artillery ammunition supplied to the BEF, was forced into a coalition with the Conservatives in May, thus ending the last Liberal government of Great Britain. All combatants consumed ammunition far faster than expected. On September 24, 1914, Joffre's headquarters had warned army commanders that ammunition would run out in fifteen days; on November 14, the German high command reckoned that it could continue fighting in Flanders for only another four days and in May 1915, British guns at Gallipoli were rationed to four rounds per gun per day. By 1915 it was clear that trench warfare had created a vicious circle. Static fighting offered more targets for guns that gulped down the ammunition, moved, with unprecedented efficiency from factory to gun-line, and at the same time demanded more high explosive (essential for demolishing defences) and less shrapnel (ideal for use against troops in the open). Combatants had to produce more high explosive, and to increase overall production on an unprecedented scale. All, in their different ways, made radical changes in the administration of their armaments industries, but, at least in the war's first years, it was existing structures that expanded in an effort to satisfy the insatiable appetite of the guns.

The British army, faced not simply with maintaining itself at mobilized strength but with carrying out an unprecedented expansion – a Third Army under General Sir Charles Monro was formed in France that summer – found things especially difficult. Sir John French, anxious not to be blamed for the failure of his spring offensives, contributed to the campaign against the government. The coalition cabinet which took over, under Asquith's leadership, was soon to include a Ministry of Munitions under David Lloyd George. Although Lloyd George emphasized his role as a radical innovator, encouraging "men of push and go," the War Office had already taken great strides in increasing the supply of munitions.

French and Joffre were united in their opinion that the Western Front deserved primacy over the Dardanelles. In view of Russian misfortunes and Italy's entry into the war on the Allied side it was essential to keep the bulk of the German army closely engaged. Passive defence would be "a bad strategy, unfair to Russia, Serbia and Italy, and therefore wholly inadmissible." Joffre then returned to his familiar plan for an attack on the flanks of the German salient, and asked the British to attack to the north of Vimy Ridge, in the mining area of Loos, to support him. Sir John French did not like the ground, but Kitchener made it clear that the French must be assisted "even if, by doing so, we suffer very heavy losses indeed." The fact that he was able to use gas went some way towards allaying French's fears, but so deep were his reservations that he kept XI Corps, the general reserve, under his own hand instead of entrusting it to Haig, whose First Army was to assault.

On September 25, the French attacked in Artois and Champagne with a flair undimmed by more than a year of war and with their way prepared by an unprecedented weight of artillery fire. But gallantry and firepower were no match for the deepening German defence, and though the French bit deep into the German first line in Champagne, a breakthrough eluded them. At Loos the British made good progress on the first day, breaking clean through the German first line, but on the second day the reserve corps, arriving too late, was massacred in front of the second line. French was censured for the late arrival of the reserves, and was replaced as commander in chief by Haig in December. A second winter descended on a Western Front, which had changed little from that of a year before. The Ypres salient was smaller, though the Allies had gained some ground in Artois and Champagne. But the French army, that good-natured burly giant, had been hard hit. It had suffered almost a million casualties to December 1914, and in the next year it lost almost a million and a half. Joffre used to say that he was nibbling away at the Germans: *Je les grignote.* At this rate, as one general warned President Poincaré "the instrument of victory is being broken in our hands."

Elsewhere, the balance of the war wobbled indecisively. Italy, lured in by the prospect of territorial gain, joined the Allies in May, and began a long series of offensives on the Isonzo. The Bulgarians, emboldened by Allied failure in Gallipoli, declared for the Central Powers, and a combined German, Austrian and Bulgarian offensive proved too much for the dogged Serbs. The Greeks, alarmed for their province of Macedonia, asked for Allied assistance, and a force was duly sent to Salonika. In 1914 a small British-Indian force landed at the head of the Persian Gulf, and in 1915, substantially reinforced, it pushed on up the Tigris, only to be checked at Ctesiphon, southeast of Baghdad, and fell back on Kut-al-Amara, where its commander, Major General Charles Townshend, determined to stand siege. On the Eastern Front the Russians began the year well by taking the Austrian fortress of Przemysl, but in May the Germans launched a major offensive, using troops shifted from the west, and by the year's end the front ran from Riga on the Baltic, past Pinsk to Tarnopol and the borders of Romania. It had been a sterile year. With hindsight its most striking features were the failure, at Gallipoli, of the war's most promising "sideshow"; the erosion of French and Russian strength; and the relentless if clumsy development of the British army into a force which would shortly make a weighty contribution to Allied strategy.

THE WESTERN FRONT

For the first winter of the war trenches were less sophisticated than they later became, although they were already assuming their characteristic "Grecian key" plan, zig-zagging, which limited the damage done by shellbursts and made it hard for attackers to work their way along them. Although what was euphemistically called "trench wastage" imposed a constant toll on units in the front line, often the most serious enemies were the climate and boredom.

ABOVE
Men of 2nd Battalion The Argyll and Sutherland Highlanders in the line, spring 1915. This unposed photograph shows a sentry keeping watch while men cook over a brazier.

ABOVE
A British 60-pdr heavy gun at full recoil
after firing, Bois Grenier, January 12, 1915.
A shortage of heavy guns bedevilled the
British for the first two years of the war.

LEFT
Territorials of the London Rifle
Brigade in the line at Ploegsteert,
south of Ypres, in January 1915.
This trench, in a relatively quiet sector,
is well provided with sleeping shelters.

ABOVE
The first Canadian troops left home in
October 1914 and eventually constituted
1st Canadian Division which went into
the line at Ypres and suffered over 6,000
casualties in the Second Battle. This
photograph shows three Canadians
emerging from the line in January 1915
after gaining experience with a British unit.

ATTACK AND DEFENCE, SPRING 1915

The British mounted a number of offensives in the first half
of 1915, notably at Neuve Chapelle in March and at Aubers
Ridge and Festubert in May. These demonstrated the need
for proper artillery preparation, something which shortage
of ammunition and heavy guns made it hard to achieve.
The Allies were themselves attacked at Ypres by the Germans
in April in the first major use of gas on the Western Front.

BELOW

This undramatic but informative
photograph shows the British front
line at Neuve Chapelle on March 10.
The ground here is too wet for a continuous
trench-line, so the British have made
sangars of earth and sandbags. German
shells are falling behind the front line to
disrupt the advance of reinforcements.

ABOVE

The British took Hill 60, southeast of Ypres, on April 17, but in May the Germans recovered it with the aid of gas. These men, gassed there, are being treated at No 8 Casualty Clearing Station at Bailleul. Wounded soldiers progressed from their Regimental Aid Post to a CCS and thence to hospital.

LEFT

Allied soldiers had no protection against gas in April, but the first respirators, goggles and pads of cotton waste, were issued to these Highlanders on May 2. The pads had to be moistened, ideally by soda water – which may be these bottles – although urine was a common alternative.

OPPOSITE

Protection against gas speedily grew more sophisticated. These men of 1st Cameronians in the Bois Grenier sector are using a Vermorel sprayer, which contained a solution of thio to absorb chlorine, to disperse gas on May 20.

ABOVE
In June the British mounted limited
attacks along the Menin road east of
Ypres. This evocative photograph shows
men of the Liverpool Scottish preparing to
assault Bellewaerde at 6 a.m. on June 16.

ABOVE
Another shot of the same action.
The flag on the right signals that
the German front-line trench has
been taken and the advance is
continuing. Men are taking cover
under the parapet of the captured trench;
the officer standing wearing a cap is an
artillery Forward Observation Officer.

THE BATTLE OF DOGGER BANK

On the night of January 28, Vice-Admiral Hipper set out for the Dogger Bank with a battle cruiser squadron, his intention being to destroy British fishing boats. The Admiralty, warned of the German plan by deciphered radio messages, planned to intercept Hipper with Beatty's battle cruisers, with the Grand Fleet in support. Hipper was duly caught by Beatty, and although *Blücher* was sunk and *Seydlitz* badly damaged, such was the British advantage that their success should have been greater. The action showed the superior quality of German gunnery, and, significantly, only a steel door closing ammunition hoists to her damaged after turrets had prevented *Seydlitz* from blowing up.

LEFT
A photograph taken from a German torpedo boat shows Beatty's battle cruisers at Dogger Bank. Beatty's flagship HMS *Lion* was badly damaged and dropped out of the line, and Beatty's cautious second-in-command failed to press his advantage.

BELOW
Hipper quite properly abandoned the stricken *Blücher*, which defended herself with "glowing courage" against light cruisers and destroyers until finished off by the battle cruisers. Here she capsizes prior to sinking.

THE FRENCH ARMY

The French Army lost almost a million men killed, wounded and captured in 1914, and in 1915 there were 1,430,000 French casualties. Most of these were incurred in repeated offensives aimed at pinching out the huge German salient that bulged out towards Noyon by attacking Artois and Champagne. But the French did learn some important lessons. Flamboyant uniforms were replaced by horizon blue (for metropolitan troops) and khaki (for colonial units), and they were the first combatants to adopt steel helmets.

LEFT
A French trench opposite La Bassée in early 1915.

ABOVE
These French North African troops,
photographed in a German prison camp
on February 6, still retain something of the
chic exquis prized by the *Armée d'Afrique*.

Wasted gallantry: French
colonial troops on the German wire.

LEFT

Despite prewar emphasis on the quick-firing
75-mm, the French were better equipped
with heavy guns that the British. Obsolete
pieces like this 220-mm mortar were
pressed into service: although they lacked
the recuperator mechanism which absorbed
the recoil of modern weapons, their heavy
shells were invaluable in trench warfare.

WAR IN THE AIR

Although both aircraft and airships were initially used only for reconnaissance, their functions rapidly widened. They were soon used to drop bombs on troops and strategic targets, and primitive fighters were developed to shoot down enemy reconnaissance and bombing aircraft, observation balloons and bombers. By the end of the war all the strands of future air power were clearly visible.

ABOVE

Flight Sub Lieutenant Reginald Warneford, the first British airman to destroy a Zeppelin. Over Belgium on June 7, he attacked one with bombs, his only weapon. Within 36 hours he received a telegram from the King awarding him the Victoria Cross. He was killed in an accident on June 17.

RIGHT

German airships, named Zeppelins after their developer, Ferdinand Graf von Zeppelin, first crossed the North Sea to bomb Britain on January 19–20, 1915. This is military airship LZ 77, which raided Essex in September 1915 and was brought down in France by ground fire in February 1916.

ABOVE
German aircraft, based in
Turkish-held Palestine, bombed
the British protectorate of Egypt in 1915.

GALLIPOLI

British and French troops, the former including a substantial Anzac contingent, landed on the Gallipoli peninsula on April 25 after the failure of a naval attempt to force the Narrows and gain entrance to the Sea of Marmara. A second landing was mounted at Suvla Bay on August 6. The crucial high ground of the Sari Bair ridge was never properly secured, and the expedition ended in failure: troops were finally withdrawn in January 1916.

LEFT

Architects of defeat? General Sir Ian Hamilton (right) with Vice-Admiral de Robeck. Hamilton, a brave and, in many respects, talented general, failed to impose the clear directing will that might have brought success either from the initial landing or the follow-up at Suvla.

RIGHT

Turkish infantry. The Turks proved resolute opponents. Their army was largely trained and equipped by the Germans, and several key appointments were held by German officers.

LEFT

A 12-inch gun aboard the battleship HMS *Canopus* engaging Turkish shore batteries during the bombardment of the Dardanelles, March 1915.

LEFT

The French battleship *Bouvet* sinks after being mined in the Narrows, March 18. Most of her crew perished.

LEFT

Unto the breach: the converted collier SS *River Clyde* shortly before running ashore at V Beach, Sedd-el-Bahr, April 25. She was packed with Munster Fusiliers and Hampshires who were to disembark from sally-ports in her sides, and Dublin Fusiliers were in the accompanying boats. They suffered terrible casualties from close-range fire.

ABOVE
V Beach, seen from SS *River Clyde*,
mid-morning. Dublin Fusiliers shelter
along a sandbank and the lighter in the
foreground is packed with wounded
Munsters. *River Clyde's* captain,
Commander Edward Unwin RN
made repeated trips in small craft
to the rock jetty to rescue wounded,
and was awarded the Victoria Cross.

ABOVE
Part of the 4th Battalion Australian Imperial Force and the mules of 26th (Jacob's) Indian Mountain Battery landing at 8 a.m. In the foreground is the staff of Colonel MacLaurin's 1st Australian Infantry Brigade. The body of an engineer, the first Australian casualty from enemy fire, lies on the beach.

BELOW
Men of 6th Battalion The Manchester Regiment attack during the Third Battle of Krithia, June 4. The village of Krithia, lying on the lower slopes of Achi Baba, dominated the exits from the Allied beachhead at Cape Helles and was repeatedly attacked but never taken.

PREVIOUS PAGE
Soldiers of the King's Own Scottish
Borderers go over the top at Helles, June 4.

BELOW
The Anzacs advanced to the spine of high
ground which runs down the peninsula,
where they were engaged in some of the war's
fiercest fighting. Here men of 4th Australian
Infantry Brigade wait on the reverse slope
behind the front-line position of Quinn's Post.

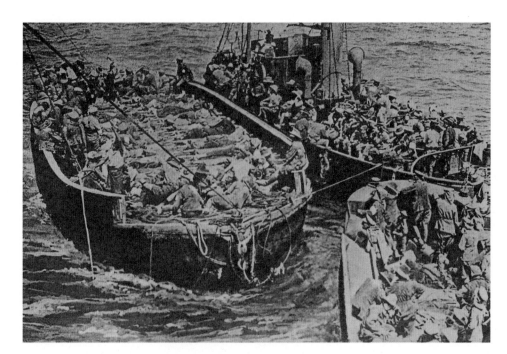

LEFT
Anzac wounded off Gallipoli.

BELOW
Well-camouflaged Turkish snipers caused great difficulties. This captured sniper has been brought in under escort. Despite the intensity of the fighting the Australians had a high regard for the Turks, known as "Jacko".

ABOVE
French infantry in the
line on the Helles front.

RIGHT
On August 21, a division of dismounted
Yeomanry attacked across a dried Salt
Lake at Suvla. This photograph shows
how the advance against well-sited
Turkish trenches was totally exposed.
One brigade lost all its staff and
seventy per cent of its officers, including
Lieutenant W. E. G. Niven, Berkshire
Yeomanry, father of the actor David Niven.

ITALY ENTERS THE WAR

Although Italy subscribed to the Triple Alliance with Germany and
Austria-Hungary, she had been edging towards Britain and France,
and in July 1914 declared that she was not bound by the terms of
the alliance, which held good only for a defensive war. Italy's
premier spoke of his country's *sacro egoismo*, and strove to get the
best terms available. After negotiations with both sides, and with
regard for the fortune of war, which then seemed to be frowning on
Austria, Italy signed the secret Treaty of London on April 26, 1915,
agreeing to join the war in return for gains at Austria's expense.

BELOW

Italy declared war on Austria on May 23:
here enthusiastic crowds celebrate outside
the royal palace in scenes reminiscent of
August 1914.

ABOVE

An Austrian infantryman on an Alpine
slope. The Italian Front is too often
neglected by historians. The adversaries
fought in some of the war's most
challenging terrain, and the Italian army
suffered appalling losses in a series of
ill-managed offensives on the Isonzo.

ABOVE
Italian ski troops. Specialist training and
equipment were invaluable for troops
operating in this unforgiving environment.

RIGHT
Dogs used by the Austrian medical services
to find wounded on the Italian front.

THE EASTERN FRONT

The year opened with the Russians successful against the Austrians in the south, but already in difficulties against the Germans in the north. In March the Russians took the Austrian fortress of Przemysl in Galicia, but the German spring offensive which began on May 1, speedily drove the Russians back. Warsaw fell on August 4, and the Germans took Brest-Litovsk at the month's end. The Tsar unwisely took personal command of his armies on September 5, but could not stop the German advance.

LEFT

A Russian infantryman in a front-line trench. Despite the ferocious hammering received by the Russian army in 1914–15 its morale did not collapse.

LEFT
Russians drag their machine guns
into captivity, Galicia 1915.

BELOW
Men of the 59th Austro-Hungarian Infantry
Regiment collecting weapons from a
captured Russian trench. The Russian
Moisin-Nagant infantry rifle was always
carried with its cruciform bayonet fixed.

A cheery German *uhlan* escorts a
column of Russian prisoners in Galicia.

GROWING BITTERNESS

In 1915 the bitterness between combatants, already fuelled by stories of German atrocities in Belgium in 1914 which lost nothing in the reporting, grew significantly. The beginning of German air attacks on Britain, the sinking of the *Lusitania* and the execution of Nurse Edith Cavell all contributed to a deepening sense of hostility which helped make compromise more difficult.

BELOW
Territorials at work clearing up debris after a Zeppelin attack on King's Lynn.

LEFT

Edith Cavell, a Norfolk vicar's daughter, was matron of a Brussels training school for nurses. She helped British and French soldiers escape to Holland, and was sentenced to death by the Germans. Shot on October 12, in her last moments she declared "patriotism is not enough: I must have no hatred or bitterness towards anyone."

BELOW

The last photograph of the fast and luxurious RMS *Lusitania*, Cunard's flagship passenger liner. On May 7 she was torpedoed off Ireland by U-20 and sank with heavy loss of life. The Germans maintained that she had been carrying ammunition, while the Allies emphasized the lack of warning and deaths of neutral Americans.

ABOVE

The sinking of the *Lusitania* provoked a
fresh wave of anti-German riots in London
and real anger elsewhere. One NCO in the
Dorsets wrote in his diary: "Surely no *man*
can read of this *Lusitania* affair without
the desire to avenge the poor dear little
kiddies and helpless women who were lost."

THE MESOPOTAMIAN CAMPAIGN

In November 1914 a British-Indian force landed at the head of the Persian Gulf, ostensibly to protect oil interests but as much to prevent Turkish agents from causing unrest among India's Moslems and encouraging Arab resistance to Turkish rule. The easy capture of Basra encouraged General Sir John Nixon and his political masters to press deeper inland, and two columns set off up the Tigris and Euphrates. Major General Charles Townshend, moving up the Tigris, took Kut-al-Amara on September 28 but lost one-third of his force in a determined attack on a strong Turkish position at Ctesiphon, only 40 kilometres (24 miles) from Baghdad, on November 22, and fell back on Kut.

ABOVE
Guns and limbers of 82nd
Battery Royal Field Artillery
are ferried across the Tigris marshes.

RIGHT
A Forward Observation
Officer of 82nd Battery controlling
fire during the advance on Kut.

THE BATTLE OF LOOS

Loos was the British army's contribution to the Allied autumn offensive and its largest battle to date. On September 25, Haig's First Army attacked with the aid of chlorine gas released from cylinders in front-line trenches. In the south, around Loos, the gas worked well and the German first position was overrun; there was less success in the north. The reserve was not committed until the morning of the 26th, and lost heavily on the German second position. The British suffered about 60,000 casualties to the Germans' 20,000. Three British major generals and the only son of the poet Rudyard Kipling were among those killed.

BELOW

The Loos battlefield seen from the British front line. The distinctive colliery winding gear known as "Tower Bridge" stood just south of Loos itself, which is out of sight to the left of this photograph. The German second position is just over the horizon, invisible to the attackers.

BELOW

On the British right 47th London Division attacked through the gas, smoke and drizzle to take a double slag-head south of Tower Bridge while 15th Scottish Division overran Loos itself. This photograph, taken by a member of the London Rifle Brigade, shows the 47th Division's attack.

ABOVE
Although this photograph is sometimes
captioned as the retreat from Mons
in 1914, it actually shows British
infantry moving through Vermelles, on
the road that bisects the Loos battlefield,
after the failure of the British attack.

FIGHTING IN AFRICA

There was sporadic fighting in Africa throughout the year.
Perhaps its most distinctive episode was the Tanganyika
expedition, when the tiny gunboats *Mimi* and *Tou-Tou* were
hauled overland to Lake Tanganyika, where they sunk their
German adversaries in December. German South West Africa
was invaded by columns marching in from South Africa and
German troops there surrendered unconditionally on July 9.

BELOW
Tractors backing downhill
with *Mimi* and *Tou-Tou*.

ABOVE

Preparing to load *Mimi* on to a steamer on the Lualaba river. As no cranes were available, the gunboats, in cradles, were hauled on to a slipway made of large tree-trunks and on to the steamer's deck.

RIGHT

General Louis Botha, South African statesman and soldier, addressing the crowd in Windhoek, capital of German South West Africa. There had been a pro-German insurrection in South Africa but it was quickly suppressed.

HITLER AND CHURCHILL

The adversaries of the Second World War both fought on the Western Front. Hitler served in 16th Bavarian Reserve Infantry Regiment throughout the war, winning the Iron Cross First and Second Classes. Churchill, who resigned from the government over the Dardanelles expedition, had been promised command of a brigade by Sir John French, but with the latter's replacement in December he was only able to obtain command of a battalion, 16th Royal Scots Fusiliers.

LEFT
Adolf Hitler (left) with members of his regiment on the Western Front.

LEFT
Winston Churchill, seen here as a major prior to assuming command of his battalion, with the French general Fayolle. Although Churchill's appointment smacked of political influence it was not wholly unreasonable: as a former regular and Territorial major he was no worse qualified for command than some "dug-outs".

A French front-line dug-out cut into
the chalk of the Ravin de Souchez,
near Vimy Ridge, October 1915.

DUG-OUTS

In British parlance the term "dug-out" meant both a former regular
officer recalled to service for the war and a deep shelter below a
front-line or support trench. Some dug-outs were hollowed out from
a trench or tunnel, while others, especially German, were created by
the "cut and cover" technique, and often had roofs made of steel and
concrete. Deep dug-outs were impervious to hits from all but the
heaviest guns. The Germans tended to take greater care over the
construction of their dug-outs than the Allies, as the latter, usually
on the offensive, often hoped that they would be on the move shortly.

ABOVE
A German company headquarters
dug-out at Wailly near Arras, April 1915.
Note the comparative comfort enjoyed
by its occupants, who have a sniper
rifle, illuminating pistol, telephone
and glass of wine to hand.

TRAINING THE BRITISH ARMY

The unprecedented expansion of the British army imposed an impossible strain on the entire training organization, which had to cope not simply with an influx of new recruits demanding basic training, but with trained soldiers who required instruction in the new techniques of trench warfare. Much of the British army's performance in the first two years of the war can only be properly understood in this context. One of the prices paid for the commitment of a well-trained BEF in 1914 was the removal of many officers and NCOs who would have proved invaluable in training a citizen army for a long war.

BELOW

The re-invention of the hand grenade, known as the Mills bomb in British service, brought with it new techniques in which bombers attacked along trenches supported by "bayonet men". Here, a bombing party of the London Rifle Brigade is under training in October 1915. A shortage of rifles means that the bayonet men are reduced to using wooden mock-ups.

BELOW

Route marches and fitness training were easy to organize. Here, men of the Queen Victoria's Rifles keep fit on London's Hampstead Heath.

BEHIND GERMAN LINES

In 1914 Moltke, who had collapsed under the strain of the first campaign of the war, was replaced by General Erich von Falkenhayn, who during 1915 generally pursued a policy of holding fast on the Western Front and attacking in the east. German defences improved steadily throughout the year, with the construction of a second position following the unpleasant shock of Neuve Chapelle in March.

OPPOSITE
An observation post in a house, July 1915. These are staff or infantry officers, for German gunners wore a ball, rather than a spike, on top of their helmets.

ABOVE
The Germans entered the war with better and more numerous medium and heavy artillery than their opponents. This 210-mm heavy howitzer, manufactured by Krupp, could send a shell weighing nearly 2½ hundredweight (127 kg) about 7,000 metres (8,000 yards).

THE COLLAPSE OF SERBIA

Serbia had already repulsed two Austrian assaults, but
when the Germans and Austrians attacked with their
new-found Bulgarian allies in October 1915 they were
hopelessly outnumbered and forced to fight with their
forces divided. Belgrade, which the Serbs had won back
after its capture by the Austrians in December 1914, fell
on October 9, and by mid-November the Serbs were in
full retreat into Albania, whence 100,000 survivors
were evacuated by the Allied fleet and taken to Corfu.

ABOVE
German hussars cross
the River Dvina into Serbia.

LEFT
Flora Sandes, daughter of a Scottish clergyman, joined an ambulance unit in Serbia and accompanied the Serb army on its retreat. Promoted to sergeant major and decorated, she remained in the Serbian army after the war, retiring as a major. She is seen here in Salonika, where many of the evacuated Serbs resumed fighting.

BELOW
Death in the snow: a dead Serb in Kosovo during the retreat, December 1915.

1916

IMPASSE

ALTHOUGH THE ALLIED TROOPS AWAITED EVACUATION FROM GALLIPOLI WHEN 1916 OPENED, IT HAD LONG BEEN CLEAR THAT THE ALLIES COULD EXPECT NOTHING THERE, AND AT CHANTILLY, IN EARLY DECEMBER 1915, THEY HAD AGREED TO MOUNT OFFENSIVES ON THE WESTERN, EASTERN AND ITALIAN FRONTS. HAIG, WHO BECAME COMMANDER IN CHIEF OF THE BEF SHORTLY AFTERWARDS, WAS TOLD BY LORD KITCHENER THAT "THE CLOSEST CO-OPERATION OF THE COMBINED ALLIED ARMIES" WAS CRUCIAL, AND SET ABOUT FORGING A ROBUST WORKING RELATIONSHIP WITH JOFFRE.

HAIG THOUGHT THE FRENCH UNLIKELY to stand another winter, believed that "the war must be won by the forces of the British Empire," and argued against the small-scale "wearing-down fights" advocated by Joffre. On February 14, he met Joffre at Chantilly and agreed to mount a major offensive that summer.

Haig was sure that the northern sector, around Ypres, offered best prospects for success, for a short advance there would drive the Germans from the Channel coast (a consideration that grew in importance with the losses inflicted by submarines based there), and seize their northern railhead of Roulers. There were compelling political reasons for the year's main offensive to take place on the River Somme, where the Allied armies now met after the southwards extension of the British front. Yet there were no good tactical objectives behind the Somme front, where an advance of 48 kilometres (30 miles) would seize little of value. It is impossible to be sure of Haig's real hopes for the battle. He told General Sir Henry Rawlinson, whose newly formed Fourth Army was to bear its brunt, to plan for a breakthrough, but the official historian, Sir James Edmonds, thought the battle "had no strategic object except attrition." It is safest to say that Haig thought that a breakthrough was possible, but even if he did not achieve one the damage done to the German army would contribute to wearing it down.

General Erich von Falkenhayn, who had replaced Moltke as professional head of the German army in September 1914, had plans of his own. Reviewing the situation in December 1915, he also concluded that France was reaching the limits of her endurance and Russia could no longer generate offensive power. Britain, the arch-enemy, was hard to attack: the terrain made Flanders an unattractive sector for an offensive against her armies, and launching unrestricted submarine warfare to throttle her nation risked bringing America into the war and would not produce swift results. Accordingly, he decided to attack France, knocking "England's best sword" from her hands, by falling upon Verdun, cornerstone of the eastern frontier, in whose defence "the French General Staff would be compelled to throw in every man they have. If they do so the forces of France will bleed to death …" Some historians, noting that the crucial memorandum exists only in Falkenhayn's memoirs and not the archives, cast doubts on the decision, arguing that this is a rationalization for a lost battle. I feel that the revisionist argument has much merit, and view Verdun as a battle launched with the aim of draining French blood.

Verdun, on the River Meuse, had been strongly fortified after the Franco-Prussian War. There were three layers of forts, arrowhead structures of concrete and steel, around the city, with their largest, Fort Douaumont, dominating a long ridge on the river's right bank. The poor performance of forts in 1914 had induced the French to withdraw most of the guns from those at Verdun, and in early 1916 the front there was quiet. On February 21, the Germans began their bombardment, with over 1,200 guns on a frontage of 20 kilometres (12 miles). The infantry attacked that afternoon, making good progress everywhere except in the Bois des Caures, in the centre, where two *chasseur* battalions under Lieutenant Colonel Emile Driant put up a determined defence. On the 25th, Fort Douaumont was taken by a small party of German infantry which took fortuitous advantage of a dislocated defence, and the whole position came close to collapse.

The day Douaumont fell General Philippe Pétain arrived to take command at Verdun. He established his headquarters at Souilly on the single road connecting Verdun with the outside world: its pivotal importance as a logistic lifeline in the months that followed was to earn it the title *La Voie Sacrée*, the Sacred Way. Pétain put new heart into the defence, and placed particular emphasis on using artillery to break up German attacks. In March the Germans switched their main effort to the left bank, and in April they attacked on both banks simultaneously, eventually taking the important features Hill 304 and the Mort Homme on the left bank and taking Fort Vaux, on the right, in a fresh assault in early June. Now the battle was turning against the Germans. The French had seized air superiority, and their guns, fire directed by spotter aircraft, took a growing toll. Falkenhayn was well aware that he was running out of time. There were unmistakable preparations for a British attack on the Somme, and on June 4 General Brusilov began a major Russian offensive, capturing almost half a million Austrians and compelling Falkenhayn to send three divisions to prop up the Eastern Front. The last German attack, on June 23, came close to success, but not close enough. The Somme offensive began on July 1, and on August 27, Romania entered the war on the Allied side. Falkenhayn stepped down to become an army commander in the east, while Hindenburg and Ludendorff returned from the East to head a German army mangled in "the Mill on the Meuse."

Verdun changed the character of the Somme. Although it remained an Allied battle, something British historians are inclined to forget, the proportion of French troops engaged dropped from roughly half to one-third. Haig came under increasing pressure to attack as soon as possible. On May 26 he told Joffre that he might not be able to do so until August, and the exasperated Frenchman declared "the French army would cease to exist if we did nothing till then." Haig had good reason to press for delay. Although Britain introduced conscription in 1916, it was the New Armies, composed of volunteers who flocked to the colours in the first months of war, who would shoulder the burden of the Somme. Though their raw material was first-rate, the New Armies were not properly trained for the battle they would have to fight. Their regimental officers were brave but inexperienced; their gunners had usually fired too little ammunition to give their observers sufficient practical skills; and the staffs at brigade, division and corps usually lacked experience of operations on this scale.

No less significant was a fundamental disagreement between Haig and Rawlinson on the character of the battle. Rawlinson favoured a methodical "bite and hold" approach, with his artillery destroying sections of the German first position – especially strong in this rolling downland with its solid villages – which the infantry could then occupy. Haig insisted on something more dramatic, which would offer the prospect of passing the cavalry of General Sir Hubert Gough's Reserve (later Fifth) Army through to exploit success.

The first day of the Somme, July 1, 1916, cost the British army 57,470 casualties. Despite an extensive artillery bombardment and the explosion of mines beneath some of the strongest points in the German line north of the Albert–Bapaume road, which bisects the battlefield, results were poor. They were better further south, in part because the French, with a higher proportion of heavy guns than the British, added their own fire to that of British guns. On July 2, Haig gave Gough command of Rawlinson's two northernmost corps and ordered the latter to press his advantage south of the road. It was not until July 12 that he had taken Mametz Wood and cleared the way for an assault on the German second position, which he attacked before dawn on the July 14 behind a short but powerful barrage. However, despite promising gains, the attack stalled on the ridgeline between High Wood and Delville Wood, and the British army, embodying strong Anzac and Canadian contingents and a smaller South African force, spent the summer in bludgeon-work in a landscape being steadily murdered by artillery.

A small number of tanks, which had recently arrived, were used in the next major attack on September 15, and by nightfall the attack had pushed deep into the German third position, within sight of Bapaume. The French steadily fought their way forward on the right, eventually cutting the important Bapaume–Péronne road. But Bapaume itself, an objective for the first week, was still in German hands when the battle ended in November. It had cost about 624,000 Allied casualties and at least as many German, the latter reflecting early emphasis on unwise counterattacks and the growing dominance of Allied artillery. One officer admitted that the Somme was "the muddy grave of the German field army, and of confidence in the infallibility of German leadership." And there is no doubt that the British army that emerged from the battle was better trained and infinitely more experienced than that which entered it. "We were quite sure that we had got the Germans beat," wrote one officer; "next spring we should deliver the knock-out blow." Yet the battle reflects British clumsiness in the handling of large-scale operations: I am not persuaded that the learning curve had to be charted with quite so many crosses. There is a particular poignancy for the Somme as far as Britain is concerned. Although some New Army divisions had fought before, it was the first time they were used on a grand scale, and casualties suffered by the locally recruited Pals' Battalions devastated local communities. The wider burden of loss was carried by the whole nation: Asquith's son Raymond, the composer George Butterworth and the writer H.H. Monro (Saki) were among those killed.

Events in some other theatres abutted on the Western Front. In March the Russians mounted an ill-starred attack at Lake Narotch in an effort to take some pressure off Verdun. And then, when an Austrian offensive into the Trentino caught the Italians, preoccupied with their own blows on the Isonzo, at a disadvantage, the Russians launched another attack to relieve them. This time the task was entrusted to Brusilov, in the southwest, and his attack, beginning on June 4 inflicted huge losses on the Austrians. But the short-term price for this success was the siphoning off of Russian troops husbanded for an attack in the centre, and in the longer term the year's fighting took the Russian army to the very end of its tether.

Romania's entry into the war on August 27 might have achieved a decisive result had it coincided with Brusilov's offensive, but there was no co-ordination with either Russian action or with a promised Allied offensive from Salonika. Although the Romanians briefly advanced into Hungary, they were speedily engulfed by Falkenhayn driving down from the northwest while Mackensen pushed up from Bulgaria. Bucharest was taken, and the remnant of the Romanian army, now reinforced by the Russians, held the line of the River Sereth, just short of the Russian border.

The Turks, encouraged by Allied evacuation from Gallipoli, were further cheered when the British-Indian garrison of Kut surrendered on April 29. A Turkish attack on the Suez Canal had failed in early 1915, and in 1916 General Sir Archibald Murray made elaborate preparations for his own offensive from Egypt into Palestine, clearing Sinai by the year's end, and preparing for an attack, early in 1917, on the main Turkish positions at Gaza.

Finally, 1916 witnessed the long-awaited clash between the Grand Fleet and the High Seas Fleet. The level-headed Vice-Admiral Reinhard Scheer took command of the High Seas Fleet early in the year, and on May 31 planned to reduce British superiority by ambushing Vice-Admiral Sir David Beatty's battle cruisers 120 kilometres (75 miles) off Jutland. The Germans had the best of the battle cruiser action, but were drawn on to the main body of the Grand Fleet. As soon as he realized this, Scheer turned away, and although the British had another opportunity of bringing the Germans to battle, this was missed because of a combination of caution, signalling errors and luck. Although Jutland was a disappointment for the British, at its end the balance favoured them even more than at its start. Jutland did not, as the British claimed, prevent the High Seas Fleet from leaving harbour again, but it did push the Germans towards what Scheer called "the crushing of English economic life through U-Boat action," and this provoked one of the most important events of 1917 – America's entry into the war.

THE BEF IN FRANCE

1916 was a crucial year for the BEF. Its new commander in chief, General (later Field Marshal) Sir Douglas Haig had just taken over, and the steady arrival of reinforcements enabled him to form two new armies, the Fourth under Rawlinson and the Reserve (later Fifth) under Gough. Ammunition was now arriving in unprecedented quantities, and the BEF fired more shells in the week leading up to the Somme than it had in the first six months of the war.

LEFT

Haig, seen here after his promotion to field marshal in December 1916. His persistence in attacking on the Western Front and his apparent disregard for the lives of his men helped make him a controversial figure after the war. The balance of history swung against him in the 1960s but it is now more even.

BELOW

A party of Territorials of 1/8th King's Liverpool Regiment at Wailly near Arras, after returning from a successful raid, April 18. The widespread use of woollen cap comforters and the occasional face blacked with burnt cork to enhance concealment in the dark gives them a piratical appearance.

MESOPOTAMIA

For the first part of the year the campaign in Mesopotamia
was dominated by attempts to relieve Townshend's garrison
in Kut. Three relief attempts failed, with the loss of 21,000
casualties, and on April 29 Townshend surrendered with 2,000
British and 6,000 Indian soldiers. General Sir Stanley Maude
replaced Sir John Nixon as commander in chief in August,
and prepared a methodical advance up the Tigris in December.

RIGHT

Fly class gunboats on the River Tigris in
early 1916. These vessels had been built
in Britain for patrol duties on the Danube,
and saw service only in Mespotamia.

BELOW

82nd Field Battery RFA on the retreat
from Ctesiphon to Kut. Six-horse
teams draw an 18-pdr gun and its limber.

ABOVE

Aircraft were used to drop supplies to the garrison of Kut, but the task was beyond their very limited capacity. Here an Henri Farman of 30 Squadron Royal Flying Corps takes off.

LEFT

Townshend (centre) and Colonel Parr, his chief of staff, with their captors. Although the Turkish commander (right) promised that Townshend's men would be "the honoured guests" of the Turks, two-thirds of them died in captivity, largely as a result of appalling treatment.

BELOW

Men of 82nd Battery RFA destroying limbers and wagons before surrender at Kut.

WAR IN THE AIR

During 1916 both sides improved both aircraft and tactics. The skies over Verdun saw an important development as the French concentrated their aircraft so as to dominate German airspace, although the pendulum swung both ways (not least because of the intervention of German ace Oswald Boelcke) before the French at last secured the advantage. This was in part due to the fact that the death of the ace Max Immelmann in June led to Boelcke being withdrawn from the line to avoid two propaganda blows in quick succession.

RIGHT

Max Immelmann, "the Eagle of Lille" gained the first official Fokker victory in August 1915 and went on to become one of the war's first "aces". He developed the Immelmann turn, a half-loop followed by a half-roll, which often placed him in an ideal firing position.

ABOVE

The Fokker Eindecker single-seat monoplane fighter had a synchronized machine gun with an interruptor which allowed it to fire through the arc of its propellor. Its introduction in 1915 gave the Germans a clear advantage which led to RFC pilots calling themselves "Fokker Fodder". This E III landed behind British lines in April 1916.

FOLLOWING PAGES

British anti-aircraft gunners run to 13-pdr guns on motor lorry mountings on the outskirts of Armentières in March 1916. Anti-aircraft fire was known to the British as "Archie", from the words of a popular song, "Archibald: Certainly Not!" The German expression Flak – Fl(eiger) A(bwehr) K(anone) – gained more lasting currency.

ABOVE

The wreckage of Immelmann's Fokker. On June 18, two FE2bs attacked three Fokkers, one piloted by Immelman, near Lens. One FE was shot down, but the other, flown by Second Lieutenant George McCubbin, attacked Immelman, and Corporal J. H. Waller, its observer, fired at point-blank range. The Germans maintained that a fault in Immelmann's interruptor had led to his own fire damaging his propellor.

LEFT

A German observation balloon about to ascend. Observers in wickerwork baskets below the balloon corrected artillery fire by telephone. Shooting down the enemy's balloons was a common task for fighters, and a side unable to use balloons because of air inferiority was at a marked disadvantage on the ground.

LEFT

Britain was raided by Zeppelins throughout 1915 and 1916, though their missions grew increasingly hazardous as RFC pilots mastered the art of shooting them down with incendiary bullets. Lieutenant William Leefe Robinson (centre) was awarded the VC for destroying Zeppelin SL11 north of London on the night of September 2–3.

LEFT

Zeppelin crews perished miserably when their airships were shot down, being killed by the flames of the burning envelope or by impact with the ground. These crew-members of SL11 lie at Cuffley in Hertfordshire.

ABOVE

Death of a Zeppelin. M. A. Edwards of Forest Road, Walthamstow, took this photograph of SL11 with a miniature German Sprite camera on September 2.

ABOVE
The metal framework of L33 at
Little Wigborough on September 23.

British troops outside the General Post Office, the rebels' headquarters in Dublin, after its recapture.

THE EASTER RISING

On Easter Monday members of the Irish Republican Brotherhood and revolutionary socialists led by James Connolly rose against the British and seized key points in Dublin. At the General Post Office Patrick Pearse, their commander, proclaimed an Irish Republic. Most Republican Volunteers outside Dublin, beset by conflicting orders, stayed at home, and although a German ship carrying arms reached Tralee Bay it was scuttled when no rebels reached it. It took the British a week to overcome the defences with infantry and artillery. Pearse and other leaders were court-martialled and executed, their deaths helping swing public opinion to support for the nationalists.

British soldiers manning a street barricade in Dublin, April 1916. Of the 450 killed in the rising, 116 were British servicemen.

LEFT

Young Frenchmen
whose age group
has become liable
for conscription
leaving Paris,
January 7, 1916.

THE FRENCH AND THE GERMANS

Although both Falkenhayn and Haig underestimated the resilience of the
French army in early 1916, it had already suffered appallingly, thanks to
repeated offensives, with well over two million casualties. Falkenhayn hoped
to finish it off completely by bleeding it white at Verdun, but discovered that
it still possessed deep reserves of determination which enabled it not merely
to contain the German attack in the first half of the year, but to counterattack
in the autumn to regain most of the lost ground. Verdun cost the French over
377,000 casualties and the Germans perhaps 337,000.

RIGHT

The French army exchanged the bright
uniforms in which it started the war for the
more sombre "horizon blue" in April 1915;
colonial troops wore khaki. It was also
the first army to adopt a steel helmet.
However, it still took regimental colours
into the field (though no longer into battle).

LEFT
French infantry attacking across
the artillery landscape, Verdun.

BELOW
British volunteer medical personnel,
many of them Quakers or others with
a conscientious objection to carrying
arms, served in *Sections Sanitaires Anglaises*
(SSA) attached to the French army.
Here, a stretcher is unloaded from an
ambulance crewed by SSA 10, attached
to the French 31st Division at Verdun.

ABOVE

The face of battle at Verdun: a German
infantryman in a ruined trench near Fort
Vaux, with a dead Frenchman beside him.

ABOVE

French transport on the *Voie Sacrée*.
When the road was running at full
capacity in June one vehicle passed
a given point every fourteen seconds.

RIGHT

A French sentry at the entrance to Fort
Vaux after its recapture, autumn 1916.

ABOVE

Allied nations routinely decorated
one another's officers and soldiers.
These French soldiers have emerged
from the line to receive British gallantry
awards. The soldier in the centre, who
has just received the Military Medal, wears
the distinctive pouches containing magazines
for the Chauchat light machine gun.

LEFT

French successes on the Somme owed much
to a superior quantity of heavy guns,
essential for demolishing German defences
dug deep into the chalk. Here, a 320-mm
railway gun reaches out into the German
rear from Etelfay on the Somme, July 21.

OPPOSITE

Both sides developed a variety of trench
artillery. Some of that used by the French
was extemporized, and included grenade-
throwing catapults. Most trench-mortars
were muzzle-loading: this breach-loader
is sited in a trench near Limey, March 5.

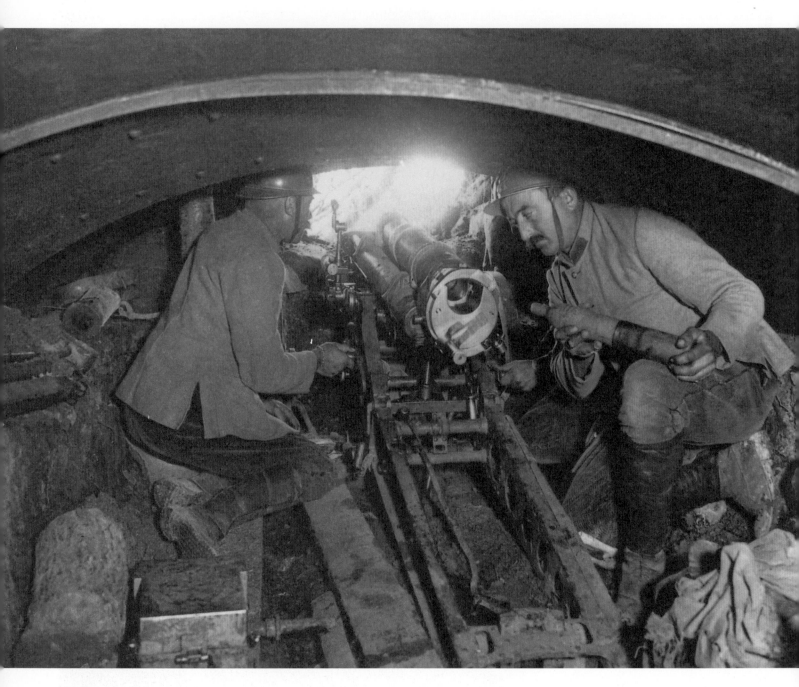

ABOVE
This 65-mm mountain gun
has been emplaced in a front-line
trench in the Argonne, May 23.

ABOVE
Senegalese infantry entraining
for the front at Fréjus, June 20, 1916.

RIGHT
Like their comrades in the infantry,
French cavalrymen exchanged splendour
for utility in 1915. These dragoons,
photographed at Booes on the Somme on
October 1, carry sword, lance and carbine.

KITCHENER AND ASQUITH

Kitchener, Britain's Secretary of State for War since the conflict's outbreak, and never comfortable in government, was in growing difficulties, though his prestige remained enormous. He was drowned when his ship was sunk at the start of a trip to Russia on June 5. Henry Herbert Asquith, Liberal prime minister from 1908, led the coalition government which took office in 1915. But he, too, floundered in 1916, with David Lloyd George, Kitchener's successor, in touch with opposition leaders and profiting from an anti-Asquith campaign orchestrated by newspaper proprietor Lord Beaverbrook. Asquith resigned in December and was replaced by Lloyd George, who established a small executive War Cabinet.

LEFT
Asquith (right) leaves the British Embassy in Paris with the ambassador, Sir Francis Bertie, March 27. Affable and courteous, Asquith stood the shocks of war well but his judicial mind sometimes allowed debate in Cabinet to meander. His son Raymond was killed with the Grenadier Guards on the Somme.

LEFT
Admiral Jellicoe bids farewell to Kitchener (the large greatcoated figure right foreground, with shoulder to camera) aboard his flagship HMS *Iron Duke*. Kitchener transferred to the cruiser HMS *Hampshire* which struck a mine off the Orkneys; there were only a dozen survivors and his body was never found.

JUTLAND

Scheer, the newly appointed commander of the German High Seas Fleet, hoped to lure part of the Grand Fleet into an ambush which would whittle away its numerical superiority. On May 31 he caught Beatty's battle cruisers, with a squadron of battleships close behind, and had the better of this part of the action. However, the British were profiting from intercepted signals, and Beatty drew him on to the massed Grand Fleet. Only a prompt German "battle turn-away" and British caution prevented a general action on terms favourable to the British. There was a missed opportunity that afternoon, when a hasty German turn and a gallant attack by battle cruisers deflected Jellicoe, and yet another that night.

ABOVE

Admiral Sir John Jellicoe aboard HMS *Iron Duke*. Described by Churchill as "the only man who could have lost the war in an afternoon," Jellicoe was cautious, partly because he knew of defects in his ships and armament. Hard-working and abstemious, Jellicoe had little in common with the flamboyant Beatty, who commanded his battle cruisers.

RIGHT

For all their majestic power, the surface warships of the age were powered by coal, and keeping their boilers at pressure was the result of constant drudgery. Worse still, these stokers toiling in the bowels of the ship would find it hard to escape if their ship sank swiftly.

ABOVE
Frederick Rutland RNAS, flying from
HMS *Engadine*, was decorated for his
valuable reconnaissance at Jutland and
was subsequently awarded the Albert
Medal for rescue work. In 1941 he was
detained under suspicion of spying for the
Japanese and committed suicide in 1949.

ABOVE

The battle cruisers at sea on the morning of May 31: Beatty's flagship HMS *Lion* leads HMS *Princess Royal* and HMS *Queen Mary*. This photograph, taken by Father T. F. Bradley, Roman Catholic chaplain aboard HMS *Tiger*, is the last one of *Queen Mary*.

LEFT

At 4.26 p.m. HMS *Queen Mary* was engaging *Von de Tann* and shooting well when she was hit by simultaneous salvoes from *Derfflinger* and *Seydlitz* and blew up, sending a pillar of smoke over 700 metres (2,300 feet) into the sky.

RIGHT

Rear Admiral Hipper ordered his battle cruisers of 1st Scouting Group to open fire at 3.48 p.m. Here, *Seydlitz* fires her first 12-inch salvo. She was hard hit (probably by HMS *Queen Mary*) shortly afterwards, but the prompt flooding of a magazine saved her from the sort of explosion that was to destroy HMS *Indefatigable*, HMS *Invincible* and HMS *Queen Mary*.

An officer aboard the cruiser HMS *Birmingham* took this photograph at about 4 p.m. *Birmingham* is on the disengaged side of 1st Battle Cruiser Squadron, led by *Lion*, which is in action with Hipper: 2nd Battle Cruiser Squadron is just visible in the left of the photograph. HMS *Queen Mary* blew up shortly after this photograph was taken.

Just after 6.30 p.m. the High Seas Fleet was partly blinded by mist and the evening sun, and receiving heavy punishment from the Grand Fleet which was "crossing the T" of the German line. But before Scheer turned away, his battle cruisers hit HMS *Invincible*, whose magazine exploded, breaking her in half.

The bow and stern of *Invincible* remained above the surface. As the battleships of the Grand Fleet steamed past her, their crews could see *Invincible* on her stern.

LEFT
Boy (1st Class) Jack Cornwell, aged 16
years and 4 months, served as a sight-setter
on a 5.5-inch gun aboard the light cruiser
HMS *Chester*. When a shell wiped out
his detachment he remained at his
post although mortally wounded, and
was awarded the Victoria Cross.

BELOW
Capably commanded by Captain Hartog,
the badly battered *Seydlitz* limped home,
despite getting stuck on the Horn Reef
as she did so. She is shown here in
Wilhelmshaven dockyard on June 6.

A LIGHTER SIDE

Even the First World War contained more boredom than
terror. Men filled their idle moments in many different ways.
"Trench art" was popular, and men made artefacts from
shell-cases, spent cartridges and the copper driving-bands
of shells. They also played cards, although gambling was,
at least in theory, forbidden in the British army.

ABOVE
German soldiers playing cards (probably
the German military favourite "skat") in a
trench at Ypres in January 1916. Note the
depth and quality of this trench, with a
machine gun, its belt stretching up from an
ammunition box, above the card-players.

ABOVE

The original caption maintains that these
soldiers of the Army Ordnance Corps are
fusing trench-mortar bombs at Ovillers, on
the Albert–Bapaume road, in September 1916.
These bombs were fired with the aid of
a metal spigot which slipped into the
mortar's barrel, and their appearance
gave them the nickname "toffee apples".

THE WAR IN EAST AFRICA

German East Africa had been annexed in 1885, and in 1914
Colonel Paul von Lettow-Vorbeck took command of the forces
there. In November 1914 he drove off a substantial British landing
at Tanga, and after another pitched battle at Jassin in 1915 decided
to adopt guerrilla tactics. In 1916 General Jan Smuts, who had
completed the capture of German South West Africa, moved
against him with two divisions, and although he was recalled at
the year's end and maintained that Lettow-Vorbeck was defeated,
in fact, the Germans remained in the field for the rest of the war.

ABOVE
Part of a South African Brigade under
Brigadier-General Beves fording the Kikafu
River on its way to Arusha, April 12, 1916.
Conditions like this wore men down, and
casualties in horses were especially high.

RIGHT
The German light cruiser *Königsberg*, off
the African coast when war broke out, was
blockaded in the Rufigi delta, where she was
photographed by a seaplane in December
1916. Her captain scuttled her, but not
before many of her guns had been removed:
they formed a valuable part of Lettow-
Vorbeck's arsenal for the rest of the war.

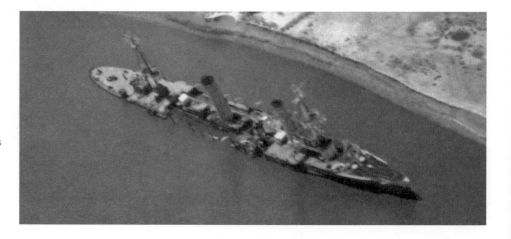

SALONIKA

In September 1915 the Allies decided to send a force to Salonika, and a multinational army, with French, British, Italian, Serbian and Russian troops, was established there in what the Germans were to call "the greatest Allied internment camp." The expedition led to acute political difficulties with the Greeks, whose territory it was, and did indeed keep a substantial Allied force committed for the remainder of the war. The front line ran through the unhealthy Vardar and Struma valleys, where malaria and paratyphoid were endemic. Maintaining the force was costly for the Royal Navy because of submarine activity in the Mediterranean.

ABOVE
General Maurice Sarrail, seen here inspecting Russian troops, was radical and anti-clerical. Dismissed from French army command in 1915, he was given command in Salonika as a sop to his political supporters. He recaptured Monastir in 1916 and in 1917 helped displace the neutralist King Constantine, who was replaced by his son Alexander with a pro-Allied premier, Venizelos.

BELOW
British troops in action, probably near Doiran in August. The Bulgarians were tough defensive fighters.

THE SOMME

The British and French planned to launch their major offensive astride the
Somme, where their armies joined. However, the German attack on Verdun
diverted French strength and encouraged Haig to attack without delay.
Although the first day of the battle, July 1, was a grievous disappointment, the
Allies gradually gained ground. On July 14 a large part of the German second
position was taken in a night attack, and on September 15 another major
assault, with the first use of tanks, bit deep into the German third position.
There was no breakthrough, but the cruel balance of attrition favoured the Allies.

OPPOSITE

The citizen army that deployed for
battle on July 1, 1916 was the finest,
in terms of its manpower, that Britain has
ever put into the field. These men of 4th
Battalion The Worcestershire Regiment,
with wire-cutters fixed to their rifles,
pause on their way to the front.

BELOW

The British plan assumed that the trenches
and dug-outs of the German first position
would have been so badly battered that
the infantry would not face serious
opposition. But there were too few
heavy guns like this 15-inch howitzer,
seen here in action on the Somme in July.

The Hawthorn Ridge Redoubt dominated the approach to Beaumont Hamel, and a mine containing 20,400 kg (45,000 lb) of high explosive was exploded beneath it at 7.20 a.m., ten minutes before zero hour. The Germans won the race for the crater, and the explosion was an obvious clue that an attack was imminent.

The Tyneside Irish Brigade (103rd Brigade of 34th Division) advancing on the axis of the Albert–Bapaume road towards La Boisselle, not long after 7.30 a.m. There was insufficient room in front-line trenches for these men, who suffered cruelly as they advanced: all four battalion commanders and all but one company commander were hit.

ABOVE

The film *The Battle of the Somme* was released while the battle was actually in progress, and was the first to show death in battle to a British audience. Some of its sequences were filmed out of the line, but others, like this still of a Vickers machine gunner, are genuine combat shots.

An 18-pdr in Carnoy Valley, near
Montauban, firing a barrage during the
attack on Pozières Ridge on July 30.
Note the abundance of live shells and
empty cases in a scene typical of a
busy gun-line on these baking
downlands before the weather broke.

Lorries delivering heavy shells from the railhead to an ammunition dump on the Somme, July 29, 1916. At the peak of a battle almost 100 trains a day brought ammunition to railheads. Some attempt has been made to camouflage the shells with brushwood.

Potential prisoners were sometimes killed in hot blood, but captives were generally well looked after near the front by men who understood what they had been through. Here British and German wounded are given what the original caption describes as water (though the container is a rum-jar) near Carnoy on July 30.

LEFT

The churchyard at Morlancourt, south of Albert and about 8 kilometres (5 miles) behind the front line, was used as an Advanced Dressing Station. This location and the trophies shown by these soldiers suggest that they were in XIII Corps's successful assault on Montauban Ridge on July 1.

BELOW

The detachment of a Vickers machine gun wearing gas masks near Ovillers. Both sides routinely used gas, which made the lives of combatants more dreadful without offering decisive advantage. This is an unposed shot: the gun's backsight is elevated for medium-range fire, and the men have spoons tucked into their puttees.

ABOVE

A front-line trench near Ovillers in July. This began as a German trench with its garrison shooting westwards, to the left: note the original firestep (with a sleeping soldier). It has been "reversed" to face eastwards by the creation of a temporary firestep, on which the sentry is kneeling, on the right.

OVERLEAF

Although this shot is well-used, it gives an unrivalled view of the British heavy guns whose growing concentration made life so nightmarish for the Germans. These are 8-inch howitzers of 39th Siege Battery, Royal Garrison Artillery, in the Fricourt–Mametz valley in August.

ABOVE
Australian gunners serving a 9.2-inch
howitzer at Fricourt: they are supporting
the attack on Pozières, which fell on August 7
at the cost of 23,000 Anzac casualties.

BELOW
Thiepval, arguably the strongest point of the
German front line, was a first-day objective
but did not fall until September 26. Here, men
of a Wiltshire battalion attack on August 7.

BELOW
Men of the Border Regiment in improvised
shelters in Thiepval Wood, August.

New Zealand infantry in their characteristic "lemon-squeezer" hats move up to the front along the Amiens–Albert road in September. The New Zealand Memorial, which stands between High Wood and Delville Wood, proudly proclaims that these men came "From the Uttermost Ends of the Earth".

BELOW

German troops on the Somme with captured British Lewis light machine guns. The heavy shoulder-belts were issued to machine gunners to help them pull guns and carry ammunition boxes, and may account for some of the stories of machine gunners being tied to their weapons: these were not the sort of men who required coercion.

ABOVE
Supporting troops moving up for the
attack near Ginchy in September 1916.
This blighted landscape is the result of
the artillery fire so copiously delivered
during the long pause on Longueval
Ridge, between July 14 and September 15.

ABOVE
Ammunition limbers moving towards
Flers past the northwest corner of
Delville Wood, September 17. In July
fighting in the wood reduced 1st South
African Infantry Brigade from 121 officers
and 3,032 men to five officers and 750 men.

Mk I Tank C19 "Clan Leslie" of
C Company, Heavy Branch, Machine
Gun Corps in Chimpanzee Valley,
September 15. Of the 49 tanks in
France that day 32 reached the start
line to participate in the attack.

ABOVE

The dug-outs of an Advanced Dressing Station at Beaumont Hamel, November 24. Attacked on July 1 by 29th Division, Beaumont Hamel was eventually taken by 51st Highland Division on November 13.

LEFT

Somme mud: artillery limbers on the Lesboeufs road near Flers, November.

LEFT

Faffémont Farm (incorrectly spelt Falfemont
Farm on British maps and the original
caption for this photograph) stood
west-southwest of Combles.
This photograph shows it on April 26,
with trenches of the German
second position running through it.

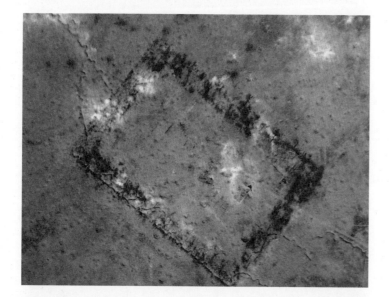

LEFT

The same farm on July 28. It is now
just on the German side of the front
line and has been extensively shelled,
partly in support of the July 14 night attack.

LEFT

The farm on September 1, in German hands
but now in the front line; it was taken shortly
afterwards. So great was the destruction
that it was rebuilt a kilometre to the east.
The battlefield graves of three members
of 1/2nd London Regiment, killed
on September 10, lie near its old site.

ABOVE

A chaplain attached to the Royal Munster
Fusiliers after conducting a field burial in
a trench. Roman Catholic chaplains needed
to be on hand to administer last rites
and were consequently often in the line:
they were generally very well regarded
by the men whose risks they shared.

THE EASTERN FRONT

Despite the losses they had already suffered, the Russians had
agreed at Chantilly in December 1915 that they would attack
in 1916 to prevent the Germans shifting troops from east to west
to face the Allies on the Somme. In March they launched a
premature attack at Lake Narotch to take pressure off Verdun,
and on June 4 Brusilov attacked the Austrians in response to
an Italian appeal for help. Brusilov's attack compelled the
Germans to move troops eastwards and encouraged Romania
to join the war, precipitating Falkenhayn's dismissal. However,
the Russians' efforts in 1916 left them fatally weakened.

LEFT
Russian cavalry on the
Galician Front in March.

RIGHT
Russian airmen standing by a Voisin LA,
1916. The Russians began the war with
about 200 French aircaft (Henri Farman,
Voisin and Blériot). Later, they also
had some huge four-engined bombers,
named after the legendary hero Ilya
Mouromets and designed by Igor Sikorski.

ABOVE

Typical Russian soldiers in what seem to
be a company headquarters. At its best, the
Russian army was very good, with tough
soldiers and an officer corps which took
its profession increasingly seriously.
However, crippling casualties, often
sustained in offensives launched to support
the Allies, sharply reduced its performance.

ABOVE
Russian soldiers ready for burial, 1916.
Although we are sometimes cynical about
the impact of religion on men in battle,
there is abundant evidence that it has
helped many to cope with war's horrors.
The proper and reverent disposal of the
dead meets a fundamental human need,
all too often denied in trench warfare.

BELOW
Austrian prisoners and Russian
soldiers at a dressing station
during the Brusilov offensive.

ABOVE
General Alexei Alexeivich Brusilov, a cavalry
officer, commanded the Eighth Army in
Galicia in 1914, and in 1916 led the
Seventh, Eighth, Ninth and Eleventh
Armies in the offensive that bears his
name. He urged the Tsar to abdicate in
1917, and joined the Red Army in 1920.

THE ITALIAN FRONT

The Italians launched repeated brave but doomed attacks on
the Isonzo front, and were caught off-balance by an Austrian
thrust into the Trentino. This provoked them to demand the
Russian assistance which took the form of Brusilov's offensive.
The year saw more sterile attrition with the soldiers of both
sides enduring conditions that were among the war's worst.

ABOVE
Italian soldiers man an
improvised anti-aircraft gun
on Monte Nero, above Caporetto.

OPPOSITE
A trench scene on the Carso front.
An Italian soldier stands on the
firestep to throw a hand grenade.

Lord Kitchener visits Italian headquarters in early 1916. General Count Luigi Cadorna, the Italian commander in chief, is the greatcoated figure on Kitchener's left, in front of the window. Cadorna was competent but unimaginative, and became increasingly pessimistic about the war.

Italian heavy guns on the move in the Piave valley. At the beginning of the war the Italians were very poorly provided with heavy guns.

ROMANIA ENTERS THE WAR

Romania was in a difficult position. King Ferdinand, who succeeded in 1914, was a cousin of the Kaiser and had two brothers in the German army, but he was married to a British princess: his government and popular sentiment alike favoured the Allies. Allied approval of Romanian claims on Transylvania and Brusilov's success persuaded Romania to enter the war on August 27. However, her army was poorly prepared and the country was invaded by Falkenhayn from the north and Mackensen from the south. The remnants of the army retired into Moldovia, and the government established itself in Jassy.

BELOW
Falkenhayn, fourth from the right, was replaced as head of the German General Staff as a result of the failure of the Verdun battle and Romania's entry into the war. But he was a considerable success when he was re-employed, as we see him here, as commander of the Ninth Army against Romania.

ABOVE
The Romanian army paid dearly for rapid
expansion from a small but good force
into a large but ill-equipped one. These
Romanian infantry have been caught in
close order by German machine-gun fire.

The entry of German and Austrian troops into the Romanian capital Bucharest, which fell on December 6. Although Romania's entry into the war was a disastrous miscalculation, she eventually profited from it. When peace was made, the country's territory almost doubled as a result of the postwar peace settlements.

1917

MUD AND BLOOD

IT WAS A YEAR OF BROKEN DREAMS. THERE WAS A REVOLUTION IN RUSSIA IN FEBRUARY, AND A COMMUNIST COUP IN NOVEMBER (OCTOBER, ACCORDING TO THE CALENDAR THEN USED BY THE RUSSIANS) LED TO AN ARMISTICE THE FOLLOWING MONTH. THE AUSTRIANS ASKED FOR GERMAN HELP AGAINST THE ITALIANS, AND THE BATTLE OF CAPORETTO WAS A MAJOR VICTORY FOR THE CENTRAL POWERS.

IN THE WEST, the Allied spring offensive failed, and the French army, worn thin by Verdun and now grievously disappointed, began to mutiny, leaving the British to bear the brunt of the war in the west. This it did, at Messines Ridge in July and then at the Third Battle of Ypres. After Third Ypres ground to its dreadful halt at Passchendaele in November, the British attacked at Cambrai, but were briskly counterattacked and lost as much ground as they had gained. Germany had briefly pursued unrestricted submarine warfare in 1915 but gave it up in the face of international protest: in February 1917 she took it up once more. It drove America into the war in April, but it would take time for American strength to make itself felt, and by the year's end it was clear that Germany must play her last card or lose the war.

Russia was in terrible straits when the year opened, her armies bled white, her ruler increasingly out of touch, her Duma (the parliament established after the Russo-Japanese War) not allowed to meet, and her cities infiltrated by agitators. In December 1916 aristocratic conspirators murdered Grigori Rasputin, whose influence on the Tsar and Tsarina they resented, but the regime stumbled on to a collapse provoked by food shortages in February and March. Nicholas abdicated in March, and the new Provisional Government, composed mainly of liberal members of the Duma, pledged to continue the war. Its task was complicated by the burgeoning of local soviets, and the arrival of exiled Bolshevik revolutionary leaders, notably Vladimir Ilyich Lenin, who the Germans allowed through their territory on a sealed train. The Russians launched their last offensive on July 1, and it fizzled out,

predictably, in blood and recrimination. Although the new premier, the socialist Alexander Kerensky, struck out against both the Bolsheviks of the extreme left and the rebellious General Kornilov, defeat at the front – the Germans took Riga in early September – and rising pressure at home were too much for him. On November 7 (October 25 in the Russian calendar, hence the "October Revolution") the Bolsheviks rose, overthrew the Provisional Government, and swiftly sued for peace.

The Austrian army had been worn down by the dual struggle against Russia and Italy. Although the casualties sustained on the Russian front were far greater than those suffered in Italy, Conrad von Hötzendorf, chief of the Austrian general staff till 1917, hated Italy, regarding its late entry into the war as treacherous. In August 1917 the Italians launched the Eleventh and last Battle of the Isonzo, and although they lost 165,000 men, the Austrians, too, were badly shaken, and Arz von Straussenberg, their new chief of staff, asked the Germans for help. This came in the form of six divisions, and on October 24 the Germans and Austrians struck at Caporetto, at the flanks of the salient created by Italians attacks. The defence soon crumbled, and there was no stopping the rout until the Piave, just north of Venice. The Italians lost about 700,000 men, mostly prisoners and deserters, and the fact that the Germans and Austrians did not push farther reflected their lack of preparation for such success. The British sent five and the French six divisions, but the Italian line had stabilized, in a remarkable display of national will, before they arrived. Caporetto initiated one significant change in Allied policy. Allied leaders met at Rapallo in

November and agreed to establish the Supreme War Council at Versailles. Although it was not a perfect war-directing body, it did mark an important step forward.

At the turn of the year, old Joffre was promoted marshal of France and kicked upstairs to a meaningless advisory post. His place was taken by General Robert Nivelle, who had succeeded Pétain as army commander at Verdun and masterminded the recapture of Fort Douaumont in October 1916. Nivelle proposed a war-winning offensive based on the methods which had worked so well there, overwhelming artillery bombardment followed by well-planned infantry assault. He wanted the British to assist by taking over the line between the Somme and the Oise, and then attacking around Arras to divert the Germans. Haig felt that he lacked the resources to comply, and in any case favoured an offensive in Flanders. But Lloyd George liked both the eloquent Nivelle and his plan, and at a conference in Calais in February he agreed to put the British army under Nivelle's command for the duration of the operation.

The Germans, meanwhile, had plans of their own. Although the winding-down of the Eastern Front allowed them to transfer troops to the west, they also planned to reduce the length of the front, and economize on the troops needed to hold it, by withdrawing to well-prepared positions known to the Allies as the Hindenburg Line. The Germans had pulled back to their new line by early April, leaving a desert of destruction behind them. They left Nivelle off balance, for they had withdrawn from part of the front he had intended to attack, and the newly liberated area required massive military support to rebuild its infrastructure. But Nivelle was determined to press on, and the attack was duly launched, in appalling weather, on April 16. It went hopelessly wrong from the start, with the Germans sitting out the bombardment in the deep caves in the limestone above the River Aisne and emerging to lacerate the attacking infantry with machine-gun fire. The offensive was called off in early May after the French had lost 100,000 men, and the conviction that the war could be won. A British liaison officer saw French wounded depressed as never before. "It's all up," they said. "We can't do it, we shall never do it. *C'est impossible.*"

From late April mutiny began to spread. It was not the result of a centrally organized conspiracy, but more like a strike, the spontaneous withdrawal of labour by citizen-soldiers who had had enough. They wanted better food, more leave, decent pay and, above all, no more crazy offensives. On May 17, Nivelle was replaced by Pétain, who set about restoring morale by a deft combination of stick and carrot. Officers who acted with "vigour and energy" against the mutineers received his full support, and many soldiers condemned by courts martial were shot, although stories of batches of mutineers being wiped out by their own artillery are exaggerated. Arrangements for leave were improved, veterans' pay was increased, and decorations were awarded to distinguished units. Pétain stopped all attacks, beginning them again only at the end of July, and then only on a reduced scale and with careful preparation. The recovery of the French army was matched by a new spirit in the government when, in mid-November, the 75-year-old Georges Clemenceau became prime minister and announced, with characteristic bluntness, "I wage war."

The British had played their part in the Nivelle plan by attacking in Artois. On April 9 the Canadian Corps took Vimy Ridge, and Allenby's Third Army jabbed eastwards from Arras behind a well-orchestrated barrage. The offensive made a very promising start, but over-reached itself, and a misguided attempt to exploit early success foundered with guns stalled too far back and communications cut. In mid-April the attack was called off after 150,000 British casualties had been suffered: this was a heavier daily loss than either the Somme or Passchendaele.

It is impossible to be sure how much Haig knew of the French mutinies, though he was aware in June that the French army was in "a bad state of discipline." He had long favoured an offensive in Flanders, and the reopening of unrestricted submarine warfare on February 1 lent impetus to this desire: that day, twenty-three of Germany's 105 operational U-Boats were based on the Flanders coast. Losses of merchant shipping jumped from around 300–350,000 tons a month in the winter of 1916–17 to 860,000 tons in April 1917. In July Admiral Jellicoe, now First Sea Lord, warned the War Policy Committee: "There is no good discussing plans for next spring – we cannot go on." In early May a conference in Paris agreed that the war-winning offensive would have to await the arrival of the Americans, but in the meantime the Allies must attack to prevent the Germans from launching offensives of their own. Haig intended to attack in Flanders, with a first blow directed at Messines Ridge, just south of Ypres, followed by a main attack out of the Ypres salient aimed at securing Passchendaele Ridge and then going on to take the railhead at Roulers and the ports of Ostend and Zeebrugge.

The attack on Messines Ridge, carried out by Plumer's Second Army, was meticulously prepared, with special emphasis on the construction of twenty-four mines loaded with a million pounds of high explosive. Elaborate artillery preparation smashed German trenches and destroyed guns, and at 3.10 on the morning of June 7, nineteen of the mines exploded with a blast that could be heard in London. Plumer's infantry overran the ridge, although their carefully phased attack meant that many of the German guns were got away. Nevertheless, it was in impressive victory. Plumer had lost almost 25,000 men but had taken over 7,000 prisoners and killed or wounded at least 13,000 Germans. Crown Prince Rupprecht of Bavaria, the German army group commander, feared that the British would follow up with a thrust for the Gheluvelt plateau east of Ypres, his main gun-line.

Gough's Fifth Army did not, however, begin its attack until July 31, and although the preliminary bombardment, which consumed 4,500,000 shells, did serious damage to German defences, it also wrecked the drainage system essential to this low-lying terrain. On the first day the advance averaged some 2,740 metres (3,000 yards), but poor weather and determined counterattacks slowed things down. Gough tried again in the second half of August, but the combination of boggy ground and well-built German pill-boxes made progress depressingly slow. For sheer horror the conditions endured by those who fought there can scarcely be excelled. Lieutenant Edwin Campion Vaughan of the Royal Warwickshire Regiment gave a heart-rending description of sheltering in a captured pill-box while "from the darkness on all sides came the groans and wails of wounded men; faint, long, sobbing moans of agony and despairing shrieks. It was too horribly

obvious to me that dozens of men with serious wounds must have crawled for safety into shell holes, and now water was rising above them and, powerless to move, they were slowly drowning."

Haig then switched the emphasis to Second Army, further south, and on September 20, Plumer made good progress, with well-planned barrages wrecking German counterattacks. Another step, on September 26, saw the Australians take Polygon Wood, and on October 4 a third step took both Second and Fifth Armies deep into the German second position. However, the appalling conditions persuaded both army commanders that the offensive should now be called off, and they told Haig so on October 5. But Haig, persuaded that the Germans were close to breaking point, ordered them to continue, and on October 9 more ground was gained in conditions that almost defy description. The last phase of the attack, which began on October 26, eventually saw the Canadians take Passchendaele, but it was not until November 10 that the battle formally ended. It had cost the British 244,879 casualties; the Germans admitted to 217,000, not including "wounded whose recovery was to be expected in a reasonable time." It had inflicted severe damage on a German army fighting in "grey desperation" with diminishing confidence in the outcome of the war. But although the British army's morale remained unbroken it had, as the war correspondent Philip Gibbs wrote, lost its spirit of optimism.

While Third Ypres was in progress, Third Army, now commanded by General Sir Julian Byng in place of Allenby, shunted off to command in Egypt, planned an attack at Cambrai, using 378 fighting tanks. A short bombardment, with targets engaged from carefully surveyed gun-positions, dispensed with the need to record targets by fire and permitted total surprise on the morning of November 20: the British captured 7,500 men and 120 guns, driving 7,000 yards into the Hindenburg Line. But in the days that followed they became drawn into a long slog for Bourlon Wood, and the German counterattack, launched on November 30, came dangerously close to cutting off the British troops in the Flesquières salient. From the Allied point of view, it was a depressing end to a bitter year.

UNRESTRICTED SUBMARINE WARFARE

Unrestricted submarine warfare involved the sinking, on sight, of merchant vessels carrying supplies to Allied nations. In 1916 pressure mounted in Germany for its resumption, although many feared that it would drive America into the war. One minister warned "If it is not trumps, Germany is lost for centuries." The German admiralty produced a study suggesting that success was certain, but Bethmann-Hollweg, the chancellor, signed the decree with regret. Unrestricted submarine warfare was resumed on February 1, 1917, and the Germans came close to starving Britain to death. But America did indeed enter the war and a variety of counter-measures checked the submarine menace.

BELOW

A surfaced U-Boat torpedoes a merchant ship. Over 15,000 British merchant seamen were lost, as opposed to the almost 23,000 of the Royal Navy, but the percentage death toll among merchant seamen was marginally higher.

ABOVE

U-35 (left) meets another submarine in the Mediterranean, spring 1917. Commanded by Kapitänleutnant Lothar von Arnauld de la Perière, U-35 sank 195 ships totalling 454,000 tons. He sank most victims with his deck gun. "We stopped the vessels," he wrote, "The crew boarded the lifeboats. We inspected the ship's documents, told the crews how they could reach the next port, and then sank the stopped prize."

BELOW

HM Troopship *Aragon* sinks in the Mediterranean after being torpedoed, December 30, 1917. A trawler stands by to assist survivors.

ABOVE

Prior to the adoption of unrestricted
submarine warfare U-Boats surfaced to
sink merchantmen, and even afterwards
shortage of torpedoes often persuaded
U-Boat captains to surface and use
their deck guns. Q Ships, like HMS
Coreopsis, shown here, were disguised
as merchantmen but mounted guns
that were unmasked at the last moment.

BELOW

A convoy zig-zagging in the Atlantic.
The Admiralty struggled hard against the
introduction of convoys, and did not
formally agree to them until April 1917.
Merchant ships were escorted by warships
which helped keep submarines at a distance
and impeded their aim, and the use of
"dazzle" camouflage confused submariners.

ARRAS AND VIMY

Haig, under French command for the duration of the 1917
spring offensive, was directed to attack at Arras to divert
the Germans from the French attack in Champagne.
The battle began well with the Canadian capture of Vimy
Ridge and British successes east of Arras, thanks in great
measure to the improvement of artillery techniques, but
soon bogged down with an exceptionally high casualty rate.

ABOVE

Artillery Forward Observation Officers
of 12th Division, one using a periscope,
direct fire from the edge of Cuthbert
crater, 3 kilometres (2 miles) northeast
of Arras, April 1917. Field telephonists
relayed messages to the guns along
cables which were vulnerable to
enemy shellfire and simple accident.

The first day's successes: captured German machine gunners lug their 1908 pattern weapon from a cellar, April 9.

Until fast and reliable light tanks were available the only arm capable of exploiting breakthrough was cavalry, whose successful use demanded speedy commitment before the defence had solidified. At Arras a British cavalry brigade was sent in near Monchy le Preux but failed to make progress; it is seen here going forward on April 13.

ABOVE
Canadian machine gunners consolidate
the capture of Vimy Ridge, April 9. The
Canadian Corps, its four divisions attacking
side by side, took the ridge in a well-handled
operation which struck a powerful chord
in Canada, inducing one author to write
that "Canada became a nation at Vimy."

THE FRENCH ARMY

The French army mutinied after the failure of the Nivelle offensive in April. This took on neither the character nor the scale of the unrest in the Russian army: men in affected units often held protest meetings and effectively went on strike, but rarely attacked officers. It was, nevertheless, profoundly serious, and it required careful handling by Pétain, who replaced Nivelle as commander in chief, to restore morale. He did this as much by improving food, accommodation and leave arrangements as by the punishment of mutineers.

ABOVE
The 313th Infantry Regiment on the march near Montigny (Marne) June 7, in the period when Pétain had abandoned offensives and was rebuilding the army's pride and confidence.

LEFT

King George V decorating Pétain with the Order of the Bath, July 12. In the Second World War Pétain became head of the Vichy-based *Etat Français*, was tried for treason in 1945 and imprisoned for life. Some Frenchmen argue that his body should be exhumed from its prison grave and moved to Verdun.

BELOW

Allied reciprocity went further than giving awards. These blinded French soldiers, both of whom hold the *Médaille Militaire* and the *Croix de Guerre*, are being given Braille lessons at St Dunstan's in London in September.

AMERICA JOINS THE WAR

Count Bernstorff, German ambassador in Washington, had warned that unrestricted submarine warfare would bring the United States, and her vast resources, into the war. Diplomatic relations were broken off on February 3, but it was not until the sinking of five American merchant vessels with loss of life, and the interception of a message – the controversial Zimmerman telegram in which Germany offered Mexico US territory in return for an alliance – that war was declared on April 6, with America pledging to use "force to the uttermost, force without stint or limit."

RIGHT

The news of America's entry into the war was an immediate Allied propaganda victory. Here, leaflets with the news, thoughtfully translated into German, are attached to a balloon, whose gas will be ignited by a burning fuse, distributing them on the German lines.

LEFT

Although the US armed forces had begun to expand before America joined the war they were still tiny: the regular US Army numbered only 133,110. There was a rush of volunteers when war broke out (here young men join the US Marines) and the government introduced conscription in May.

ABOVE
"Over There": US troops march down
London's Piccadilly on August 15. Scenes
like this gave a fillip to British morale as
Third Ypres ground on and German
submarines ravaged merchant shipping.

LEFT

The US commander in chief General John J. "Black Jack" Pershing stands beside Marshal Joffre at the Invalides on July 4. Pershing demanded an army of a million men by 1918 and three million a year later, and emphasized that it would fight as an American army, not with its men split up among the Allies.

BELOW

Another shot heard round the world. The first American field gun to fire in France: it is, in fact, a French designed 75-mm of 6th Field Artillery.

GERMAN WITHDRAWAL
TO THE HINDENBURG LINE

In March the Germans shortened their line on the Western Front by withdrawing from the nose of the great salient that bulged out towards Paris to a well-prepared position called the Hindenburg Line by the Allies and the *Siegfried-stellung* by the Germans. Territory relinquished was devastated in an operation named after Alberich, the spiteful dwarf in the *Nibelungen* saga. The German withdrawal wrong-footed Nivelle, part of whose offensive had been aimed at ground now given up, and left the Allies with a massive task of repair.

ABOVE

The village of Serre, on the northern end of the Somme battlefield, was fruitlessly attacked in 1916, most notably by the Accrington Pals and the Sheffield City Battalion on July 1. It was given up when the Germans withdrew in March 1917, as these jubilant British soldiers testify.

ABOVE

The Duke of Lancaster's Own
Yeomanry crossing a temporary
bridge over the Somme at Brie, near
Péronne, in March. Destruction like this
was comprehensive across the area given
up; Ludendorff even gave specific orders
to destroy the castle at Coucy le Château,
the finest medieval fortress in France.

THE AIR WAR

The war in the air continued to develop, with both sides recognizing the importance of winning air superiority over key sectors of the front so as to deny the enemy reconnaissance and artillery spotting, and its aircraft reaching deep to attack targets like ammunition dumps. In 1917, aircraft took over strategic bombing tasks from more vulnerable airships. Aces did not simply cause disproportionate loss, but also generated publicity in nations that were becoming increasingly war weary.

ABOVE
A German Fokker D lies wrecked on Pilckem Ridge on July 31, the first day of the Third Battle of Ypres. The damage suggests that the machine has been brought down by an anti-aircraft shell.

RIGHT
Captain Georges Guynemer receives the *Légion d'Honneur*. His boyish looks and chivalry (he once spared Ernst Udet when his ammunition ran out) made him France's most famous ace, although, with 54 victories, he ranked second to René Fonck with 75. He disappeared at Poelcapelle in the Ypres salient, aged 24.

LEFT
Bombing developed steadily. In August 1914 Lieutenant von Hiddessen became one of the first aviators to attack a town when he dropped three bombs on Paris. The twin-engined three-seater Gotha bomber seen here took over the task of bombing Britain from the more vulnerable Zeppelins.

BELOW
London's Central Telegraph Office blazes after being hit in a daylight Gotha raid on July 7.

ABOVE
The measured and skilful Major James McCudden served as a gunner and observer before returning to France as a sergeant-pilot in July 1916. He was Britain's second highest-scoring ace, with 54 victories to Edward Mannock's 73, and was accidentally killed in July 1918, shortly after winning the Victoria Cross.

THE HOME FRONT

By 1917 the war industry of all European combatants was working at full capacity. The fact that so many men were away at the front, coupled with the unprecedented demand for workers, drew women not only into war production but also into a host of other areas traditionally regarded as male preserves. They even appeared in uniform, and although their services remained distinct, they served abroad in a variety of roles, many unlike women's traditional functions, such as nursing.

BELOW

The interior of a tank factory in 1917. Although the British army of the First World War is often regarded as irredeemably conservative, it not only pioneered the use of tanks on the Somme in 1916 but was the first to use them on a large scale at Cambrai in November 1917.

ABOVE
Coventry Ordnance Works producing heavy
naval guns. Gun barrels wore out with use,
and in the background a naval gun is being
hoisted in to have its barrel relined, probably
as a result of use at Jutland in 1916.

ABOVE
Women munitions workers guiding shells
moving along an overhead gantry at the
national shell-filling factory at Chilwell,
near Nottingham in July 1917. For much
of Third Ypres British gunners fired 500,000
shells a day, almost twice as many as during
the whole of the Boer War of 1899–1902.

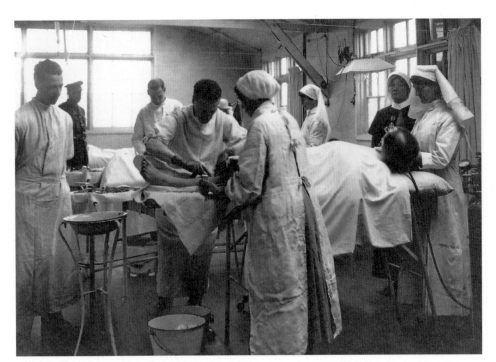

LEFT

An operation at No. 34 Stationary Hospital at Wimereux. The surgeon, Colonel Fullerton, is assisted by a female theatre sister and two female anaesthetists.

BELOW

An officer of the Women's Royal Naval Service (WRNS, or Wrens for short) training army recruits in respirator drill. Such an authoritative role would have been impossible for women before the war.

LEFT
A woman train driver on
Canada's Northern Pacific
Railway, October 1917.

BELOW
Much war work was anything but
glamorous: these women are sorting
coal in the yard of a gas-works and
then wheeling it to the furnaces.

LEFT

Women of the Forestry Corps load logs on to a horse-drawn sledge at Cross-in-Hand, near Heathfield in Sussex.

BELOW

The Allied blockade of the Central Powers was cutting deep into food supplies by 1917, and in April there were strikes against the reduction of the bread ration. Here, a woman serves food from a mobile cooker, the "goulash gun", in a working-class suburb of Berlin.

THE BATTLE OF MESSINES RIDGE

Messines Ridge, south of Ypres, had been taken by the Germans
in October 1914 during the First Battle of Ypres. The British
had begun work digging mines beneath it shortly afterwards,
and in June 1917 these were used as part of a carefully prepared
attack on the ridge by Plumer's Second Army. An accurate
preparatory bombardment had destroyed many German guns
and smashed trenches on the ridge, and the infantry, moving on
timed phase-lines to preserve control, took all their objectives.
Some German observers, however, thought that British tactical
methods were more ponderous than those of the Russians.

ABOVE
It was entirely characteristic of the
painstaking Plumer that troops were briefed
on a scale model of the ground over
which they would fight. Here British
soldiers (foreground) and Australians
(in slouch hats) study a model
between Nieppe and Petit Pont, June 6.

ABOVE
Although Messines Ridge was commanding
ground, the Germans holding it were
pitilessly exposed to British artillery
observers. This view across the Douve
valley shows British shells falling
on Messines in early June.

ABOVE

The village of Wytschaete on Messines
Ridge after its capture on June 7 by men
of 16th (Irish) and 36th (Ulster) Divisions.
There was no conscription in Ireland
during the war, but Irish soldiers played
a notable part in it, some serving in
Irish Regiments and others in British
regiments which, like the King's Liverpool,
traditionally had a substantial Irish content.

RIGHT

A German prisoner captured on Messines
Ridge. The bags beneath his eyes and the
heavy growth of beard testify to the misery
of living under the bombardment, but
he seems understandably glad to be alive.

THIRD YPRES

The Third Battle of Ypres, often known as Passchendaele, from what is strictly the name of one of its component battles, was fought in an effort to capture Passchendaele Ridge, take the German railhead at Roulers and seize the ports where some German submarines were based. It was launched by the Fifth Army on July 31 but progress was poor, in part because of an unseasonably wet summer. Second Army took over the main responsibility in August, and by November, the British had seized Passchendaele Ridge after a battle that remains a byword for endurance in nightmarish conditions.

ABOVE

German prisoners awaiting interrogation during the Battle of Pilckem Ridge, the first stage of Third Ypres, on July 31. The standing German wears a cuff-title awarded to his regiment's Hanoverian forebear for service with the British during the siege of Gibraltar in 1780–83.

RIGHT

Tending wounded in an Advanced Dressing Station near Ypres.

The Battle of Menin Road Ridge, one of Second Army's successful assaults. 13th Durham Light Infantry preparing to attack Veldhoek, September 20.

BELOW
Cause: a 9.2-inch howitzer of the Australian 55th Siege Battery in action at Voormezeele, September 13. Note the camouflage net to aid concealment from the air.

ABOVE
And effect: the low-lying terrain of much of
the salient broke up because of the impact
of shelling, the destruction of the drainage
system and unusually wet weather.
Here, gunners strive to pull their 18-pdr
from the mud near Zillebeke, August 9.

The abomination of desolation: Canadian stretcher bearers bringing in wounded at Passchendaele, November 14.

Captured German officers outside their concrete bunker, near Langemarck, on the northern edge of the salient, October 12. These structures resisted hits by all but the heaviest guns, and had to be taken by assault. They still dot the Flanders landscape, and are sometimes used to house cattle or as tool sheds.

ABOVE
Captioned as "the interior of a dug-out"
near Ypres, November 2, 1917,
this photograph probably shows
the interior of a German pill-box put
into use, as so many were, by its captors.

ABOVE

Several factors, of which discipline was
but one, got men through the ordeal of
Passchendaele. Regular leave gave them
something to look forward to, although it
was sometimes curiously unsatisfactory,
as men felt reticent about discussing
their experiences with their families.
Here, soldiers queue to change
money at a London terminus.

CAMBRAI

The attack at Cambrai had mixed parentage: the Tank Corps sought to show its prowess on suitable ground, and Brigadier-General Tudor had developed a system for the silent recording of artillery targets. On November 20, 378 fighting tanks with abundant infantry bit deeply into the Hindenburg Line. But 179 were lost on the first day, and the British became bogged down in a battle for the dominant Bourlon Wood. A German counterattack, making good use of the developing storm-troop tactics, snapped in against the shoulders of the new salient on November 30, and British losses, at around 45,000 men, eventually equalled those incurred by the Germans.

BELOW

This aerial view of the Battle of Cambrai gives a good impression of the trenchscape so characteristic of the Western Front, with the zig-zag "Grecian key" design of trenches and a world laced by shellbursts and fires.

BELOW

Many tanks lost were ditched or broke down. Here Hyacinth, a tank of H Battalion, Tank Corps, has failed to negotiate a German second-line trench a kilometre west of Ribecourt, in the centre of the battlefield. Men of 6th Division's 1st Leicesters look on.

ABOVE
A tank of C Battalion, Tank Corps, tows a
captured German 5.9-inch gun through the
wood east of Ribecourt, November 20.

ABOVE

Battle traffic, November 22. Getting cavalry
through crowded rear areas made it hard
to exploit initial success, although the
Canadian Cavalry Brigade advanced
13 kilometres (8 miles), capturing 400
men and nearly 100 machine-guns.

GERMAN EAST AFRICA

In 1917 Lettow-Vorbeck continued his epic struggle in German East Africa, fighting a sharp battle at Kissaki and then moving down the Rufiji valley. He beat off a determined attack by British West African units in October, and at the year's end set off, having left behind most of his wounded, up the Rovuma valley, the border between German East Africa and Portuguese East Africa (present day Mozambique). A providential attack on a Portuguese garrison gave him enough supplies to continue the campaign into 1918.

ABOVE
Lettow-Vorbeck (second from right) with some of his staff. He fought on until given news of the armistice in 1918. He returned to Germany to a hero's welcome but lost both his sons in the Second World War; he was joyfully greeted by his surviving askaris when he visited Africa in 1964.

BELOW
One of the guns from *Königsberg*, mounted for the defence of the town of Mwanza, immediately after its capture.

ABOVE
Indian gunners of the Kashmir
Mountain Battery in action at
Nyangao, October 16–18, 1917.

LEFT
HMS *Severn* working close inshore
to provide fire support at Lindi,
June 10, 1917; her fire control top
has been masked with foliage.

FOLLOWING PAGE
Both sides in East Africa relied greatly on
locally recruited soldiers. Here, a patrol
of 4th King's African Rifles pauses by
a badly wounded German askari.

THE ITALIAN FRONT

The Italian army had battered repeatedly against strong positions
in appalling country: a high proportion of wounded were blinded
by the effects of shellfire on rocks. Italian gains in the 13th Battle
of the Isonzo persuaded the Austrians to ask for German help,
and the arrival of German troops enabled the launching of a
two-pronged attack at Caporetto. The defence folded rapidly,
but the attackers were not sufficiently prepared to capitalize
on their success, and the Italians rallied on the line of the Piave,
just north of Venice. British and French troops were sent to
Italy and remained there for the rest of the war.

BELOW
Italian Alpini carry supplies up a snowy pass.

ABOVE

This classic photograph of General Otto
von Below's battle headquarters at
Caporetto shows the commander and
his staff operating with an insouciance
which would not have been wise elsewhere.
A pennant marks their location, a
tripod-mounted range-finder stands
ready, and a telephone detachment
(right foreground) relays information.

ABOVE
Italian prisoners taken at Caporetto.

MESOPOTAMIA

British and Indian troops under the command of Lieutenant General Sir
Stanley Maude resumed their advance up the Tigris in strength in
December 1916, recaptured Kut in February and entered Baghdad in
March. Maude then sent three columns up the Tigris, Euphrates and Diyala
rivers to prevent any prospect of Turkish counterattack, and each won
useful victories. Maude died of cholera in November, and his successor,
Lieutenant General Sir William Marshall, continued the advance.

LEFT
Turkish prisoners
taken during
Lieutenant General
Maude's advance.

RIGHT
Indian infantry re-occupy Kut-al-Amara,
scene of the British capitulation in 1916.

BELOW
Officers and men of 1/4th Battalion,
The Hampshire Regiment, a Territorial
battalion, make their formal entry into
Baghdad on March 11 to constitute the
city's garrison.

PALESTINE

In 1916 the British moved into Sinai, and in March the following year launched the first of their attacks on a strong Turkish position running through Gaza to the sea. The attack failed with loss, and a second attempt in March was no more productive. These unimaginative battles saw Murray replaced as commander in chief by Allenby, who soon displayed an affinity for mobile warfare. In October he fixed the garrison of Gaza by a frontal threat and then outflanked the position by a sweep through Beersheba with his mounted units. The battle was a substantial Turkish defeat, and left Jerusalem within Allenby's grasp.

Officers conduct a burial service for members of 1/4th Northamptonshire Regiment, killed at First Gaza. This stark photograph shows the sort of trench burial common when large numbers of bodies had to be interred quickly. The Imperial (later Commonwealth) War Graves Commission shows trench burials by placing headstones so that they touch.

LEFT
T. E. Lawrence had visited the area as an archaeologist, and after serving on the intelligence staff in Cairo was sent to liaise with Sherif Husain of Mecca, leader of a revolt against the Turks. Lawrence showed his regard for the Arabs by wearing their dress, to the irritation of his superiors, and though his role was inflated, it was nonetheless important.

RIGHT
The triumphal entry of the Arabs into the Red Sea port of Aqaba on July 6, 1917.

BELOW
13-pdr guns of 20th Brigade Royal Horse Artillery of the Yeomanry Mounted Division crossing the Wadi el Saba near Beersheba in October.

LEFT
Men of 3/3rd Gurkha Rifles,
75th Division, kneel on the firestep
ready to go "over the top" in December.

RIGHT
The mayor of Jersualem set off with
a surrender party early on December 9,
and found, not the senior officer he sought,
but Sergeants Hurcombe (right) and
Sedgwick (left) of 1/19th Londons, who
cheerfully accepted the city's surrender.

SALONIKA

Allied strength in Macedonia (or Muckydonia as the British called it) increased to more than 500,000 men, although the prevalence of disease meant that relatively few were available for duty. There were unsuccessful Allied offensives at Lake Prespa in March and on the Vardar in May. In June King Constantine abdicated under Allied pressure. Greece entered the war on the Allied side on June 27, and Sarrail's successor, General Marie-Louis Guillemat, who took over in December, set about integrating the Greeks with the other Allied contingents. It was not, however, until September 1918 that the Allies launched a major offensive from Salonika, reaching the Danube the day the war ended.

ABOVE

A Scottish sentry guards Salonika harbour.

LEFT

The war continued to interweave ancient and modern: here a French Henri Farman flies over British lancers.

TURKEY

Like its allies and opponents, Turkey too was wilting under the strain of the war. Victory in Gallipoli and at Kut was more than counterbalanced by the defeats in Mesopotamia and Palestine in 1917. However, the collapse of Russia encouraged Enver Pasha, the war minister, to expand eastwards and regain territory lost in 1878. This was eventually to bring the Turks into conflict with German satellite states and imperil the German-Turkish alliance.

ABOVE
Ox-drawn Turkish heavy guns on the march. Although the artillery enjoyed high status in the Turkish army, it was patchily equipped. For Turkey the war formed part of an almost continuous conflict, beginning with the first Balkan War in 1912 and ending in 1922 after the war against Greece. In the process the population of Anatolia fell by 17.7 percent, and the sufferings of "Little Mehmet", the ordinary Turkish soldier, were legion.

RIGHT
Enver Pasha is shown a film camera in May 1917. A leading member of the "Young Turks", Enver played a key role in bringing Turkey into the war. He was a failure as a field commander, and his involvement in outrages against the Armenians has further tarnished his reputation. He was killed leading anti-Soviet rebels in Uzbekistan in 1922.

THE EASTERN FRONT

The Russian army had spent its strength by 1917, often in offensives launched at the behest of the western Allies and intended, like the Brusilov offensive of 1916, to take the pressure off the Western Front. Russia remained in the war after the Tsar's abdication, and launched her last major offensive in Galicia in July. Not only did this fail hopelessly, but the Germans took Riga in September in a brilliant demonstration of the efficacy of a lightning bombardment combined with storm troops.

BELOW
Ensign Walter Beck of the Austro-Hungarian 74th Infantry Regiment took this photograph showing a machine-gun position, probably in the Wolhynian Marshes, in early 1917.

LEFT
Field Marshal Prince Luitpold of Bavaria, commander in chief on the Eastern Front (fourth from right) with his chief of staff Major General Max Hoffman (author of German victory at Tannenberg in 1914) second from right, during the capture of Tarnopol, July 24.

OVERLEAF
Russians break and run in Galicia.

ABOVE

Despite scenes like that in the previous
photograph, the Russian collapse was
not total, and the army did not, as Lenin
was to maintain, "vote for peace with
its feet" until November. There is a good
measure of order in this retreating column,
and the Russian artillerymen (furthest
from camera) have stood by their guns.

RIGHT

Delegates of the Central Powers arrive
for peace negotiations at Brest-Litovsk,
December 20. The Austrian foreign minister,
Count Czernin, wearing a cap, faces his
German opposite number, Kuhlmann.
The latter had spent several years in
the London embassy, and during indirect
peace negotiations in mid-1917 favoured
the unconditional return of Belgian
territory to encourage Britain to settle.

THE RUSSIAN REVOLUTION

In March, shortages of food and fuel combined with
deep war-weariness, lack of confidence in the government
and revolutionary agitation to provoke a revolution that
saw the establishment of the Soviet of Soldiers' and Workers'
Deputies, provoked the abdication of the Tsar. The new
Provisional Government, led from July by the socialist
Alexander Kerensky, strove to remain in the war. Defeated
at the front and undermined at home, it was itself toppled
by a coup engineered by the disciplined minority of Bolsheviks
in November. Lenin moved swiftly to dissolve the Constituent
Assembly, initiating the "dictatorship of the proletariat."

BELOW
In March, all military units were ordered
to elect rank and file representatives to the
Soviet. Officers speedily lost their authority,
and an attempted coup by General Kornilov,
who became commander in chief in July,
accelerated the spiral into indiscipline.

ABOVE

In March the Provisional Government raised
"Battalions of Death" composed of women
soldiers. These were designed to shame men
into continuing with the war and to send
a clear signal of Russian resolve abroad.
Photographs like this were widely reproduced
in the West, which was used to seeing
women in uniform but not bearing arms.

ABOVE

The revolution in Petrograd (formerly
St Petersburg, renamed in 1914 to
sound less German): students and
soldiers firing at the police, November 16.

RIGHT

Iconoclasm: symbols of the
old regime are removed from
the Duma building, November 16.

1918

ARMISTICE

ON NOVEMBER 11, 1917, LUDENDORFF PRESIDED OVER A CONFERENCE OF GERMAN STAFF OFFICERS IN MONS. THEIR DELIBERATIONS WERE NOT PURELY MILITARY, FOR THE DUUMVIRATE OF HINDENBURG AND LUDENDORFF WAS THE DRIVING FORCE IN GERMANY. THE "DEFEATIST" CHANCELLOR BETHMANN-HOLLWEGG HAD BEEN REPLACED BY MICHAELIS, WHO HAD NOW BEEN SUCCEEDED BY HERTLING: THE GENERALS PROPOSED AND THE GOVERNMENT CONCURRED.

LUDENDORFF WAS NOT ENCOURAGED by the situation. The blockade was biting hard on Germany, where food shortages provoked growing unrest. Austria still struggled on, though she was demonstrably at the end of her tether. Turkey was in retreat in Palestine and Mesopotamia, where the British continued to advance: and, although Ludendorff could not yet have known it, was about to divert much of her declining strength to the Caucasus. On the credit side Russia was effectively out of the war, even though peace was not to be made at Brest-Litovsk till March 1918. But if Britain and France were both down to the last reserves of their manpower, the enormous demographic and industrial resources of the United States would shortly make themselves felt. America's entry into the war had changed the whole strategic balance. If her strictly military contribution was to prove less significant than that made by existing Allied combatants, she had already given an enormous fillip to morale. And recognition that her burgeoning strength would eventually prove decisive persuaded Ludendorff that, one way or another, he had to end the war in 1918.

Germany had two options. She could seek to make peace, choosing a moment when the military balance seemed tilted in her favour, with a declaration that she had no claims on Belgium as a useful preamble. This was to become significantly harder after US President Wilson's Fourteen Points of January 1918 established far harsher preconditions, including the return of Alsace and Lorraine to France. The alternative was to capitalize on Russia's exit and

strike a terrible blow on the Western Front, knocking France and Britain out of the war before the American Expeditionary Force (AEF) was present in strength. Temperament helped drive Ludendorff towards making this gambler's throw, and if, in retrospect, he must be criticized for embarking upon a strategy that left Germany in a far worse position than would have been the case had she pursued tentative peace offers in 1917, it must be acknowledged that he came within a hair's breadth of achieving military success.

Ludendorff and his advisers agreed that they must attack. But where should the blow fall? Beating the French would be likely to leave Britain in the war, and an undefeated Britain, backed by the United States, could still maintain the blockade. Ludendorff concluded that "we must beat the British." At one level the destruction of the British army in France might provoke a collapse of public support for the war, while at another a British defeat on the northern flank would be likely to unhinge the French position too. Ludendorff's staff produced a variety of plans. "George I" and "George II" would cut in either side of Ypres, while "Mars" and "Valkyrie" aimed at Vimy and Arras. Further south, "Michael III" would head for Bapaume, "Michael II" for Albert and "Michael I" for Péronne. Frustratingly, although the northern options offered the best prospect for long-term success, as the important British railhead of Hazebrouck was close to the front and the Channel ports were not far behind it, it was precisely in this sector that a breakthrough would be hardest to achieve. The Passchendaele battle had shown just how difficult the Ypres salient had become, and an attack around Arras would have to cope with the bastion of Vimy Ridge. Ludendorff accordingly decided on the "Michael" offensives, with the hope of breaking the front and then swinging right to carve through the British rear. He spoke at the time of knocking a hole and letting the rest follow, and modern research has shown that he was indeed opportunistic: it seems unlikely that, for instance, he appreciated the importance of Amiens as the crucial rail link between the British and French armies.

Although all combatants had been experimenting with specially trained assault infantry, it was the Germans who had developed the concept most fully. In 1915 Captain Willy Rohr commanded a unit composed of section-sized "stormtroops", supported by machine guns, mortars and flame-throwers. Assault detachments were expanded after Verdun, and soon the "princes of the trenches", the keenest and fittest of Germany's soldiers, using the latest weapons and tactics, played the leading role in attacks. General Oskar von Hutier used them to capture Riga, and the counterattack at Cambrai was spearheaded by stormtroops, supported by assault pioneers, who pressed on through gaps in the British defence while conventional infantry followed to mop up pockets of defence.

The artillery support for stormtroops had been developed by Georg Bruchmüller, a retired lieutenant colonel in 1914, who had quickly risen to eminence and gained the nickname "Durchbruchmüller" – "break-through Müller". His meticulously organized artillery orchestra prepared the way for attacks with a short but exceptionally severe bombardment, with the full depth of the defender's position being methodically hammered before the creeping barrage moved just ahead of the infantry. The latter were accompanied by their own trench mortars and close-support guns. Bruchmüller had seen just how effective the silently prepared British barrage had been at Cambrai, and managed to get a similar system partially adopted by his own army.

The British, upon whom this blow was to fall, were below strength. On March 1, Haig's infantry was a little over half a million strong, just 36 per cent of his strength rather than the 45 per cent it had been six months before. Growing numbers of teenagers filled the ranks, and in April 1918 conscription was extended to include men aged 41 to 50. Worse, by January 1918 the British had extended their front to the River Oise, taking over another 67 kilometres (42 miles) from the French, much of it consisting of trenches that were well below standard. At the same time the British were adopting a defensive layout based on the German system of a thinly held Forward Zone, a Battle Zone that provided the main line of resistance, and a Rear Zone protecting supply dumps. Gough's Fifth Army, on the southern end of the front, had only 18 divisions to hold 67 kilometres, and far too few labourers to bring its sketchy defences up to scratch. Worse, the changes had not been fully thought through, and there was resistance to the notion of holding the Forward Zone with isolated redoubts whose machine guns covered the ground between them. "The British Army fights in line," grumbled one seasoned NCO, "and won't do any good in these bird cages."

The logic which drove Ludendorff to attack was not lost on the Allies, and the German offensive came as no surprise. But this was scant comfort to the troops manning positions hit by three million shells early on the morning of March 21. Trenches were flattened, batteries smashed and even deep telephone cables exhumed. And it was a foggy morning, so that the stormtroops slipped like wraiths through gaps torn in the Forward Zone. Some units fought with grim determination, but by nightfall the Germans had made good progress, inflicting over 38,000 casualties, 21,000 of them prisoners. As the Germans drove on, there was growing gloom in the Allied high command. Haig feared that he was bearing the weight of the attack alone, while Pétain suspected that the British were close to defeat. On March 26 Allied leaders met at Doullens, within earshot of the front, and agreed that Ferdinand Foch would co-ordinate the efforts of their armies.

In fact, the German attack was already losing momentum, partly because it was outreaching its logistic support, and partly because it proved impossible for German commanders to stop their men gorging themselves on captured food and drink. The near collapse of the Fifth Army cost Gough his job: he was replaced by Rawlinson, and the troops now consolidating in the face of the slackening assault became the Fourth Army. The Germans were at last halted at Villers-Brettonneux, within sight of Amiens.

With "Michael" stuck fast, on April 9 Ludendorff triggered "Georgette", a modified version of "George", catching an over-extended Portuguese division in front of Neuve Chapelle and going on to take a deep bite out of the British line, swallowing all the hard-won gains of Third Ypres. In late May he struck again, this time on the Chemin des Dames, where he mauled the French Sixth Army and a British corps, which was serving under its command in a sector hitherto so quiet that it was known as "the sanatorium of the Western Front." As the Germans exploited, they ran into the Americans. Pershing, their commander, was insistent that his men should fight as a cohesive whole, but was prepared to heed Foch's request and support the sagging front. On June 3 machine gunners of the US 3rd Division checked the Germans at Château-Thierry on the Marne, and later that month US Marines took Belleau Wood after a battle that revealed both tactical innocence and very real determination. Ludendorff tried again in June and in July he launched his final effort in Champagne. Officially named the "Reims-Marneschutz", it was known at the *Friedensturm* – the "Peace Offensive" – for Ludendorff was now striving to persuade his men to gain bargaining counters for a compromise peace, rather than win the total victory which had beckoned in March.

The Ludendorff offensives had driven huge salients into the Allied line, but had cost the Germans more than a million men, and the loss fell heaviest on the bravest and the best. The Allied riposte began with a French counterattack in July, with Mangin striking around Compiègne, and on August 8 the British launched a major attack east of Amiens, with the Anzacs, Canadians and a British corps, lavishly supported by tanks, forcing the Germans back for 12 kilometres (8 miles) on what Ludendorff called "the black day of the German army in the war." *"Tout le monde à la bataille,"* ("Everybody to battle") declared Foch, as the Allies pressed forwards in two mighty thrusts.

In the east Pershing's men, who had pinched out the salient at Saint-Mihiel, south of Verdun, in mid-September, attacked into the forest of the Argonne, striking parallel with the Meuse across ground

that might have been made for defence. By early November they had reached the little town of Sedan, scene of a major German victory in 1870. In the northwest the British attacked towards Cambrai, elbowing their way through the Hindenburg Line in late September to reach Mons, where the BEF had fired its first shots in 1914, on November 10. The last hundred days of the war cost the British some 300,000 casualties, but in the process they captured twice as many prisoners as the Americans, French and Belgians put together. It was a formidable achievement, all too often ignored by those who see Britain's contribution to the war as one of unrelieved failure.

As the Allied armies drove inexorably onwards, so the German political base crumbled. On September 14 she made Belgium a peace offer, and two days later Austria suggested "confidential and non-binding" discussions on peace terms: both proposals were rejected. Bulgaria signed an armistice on September 29, and that day Ludendorff's nerve broke at last. On October 2 his emissary told the party leaders of the Reichstag that there was no longer any prospect of forcing the Allies to agree to peace. Prince Max of Baden became chancellor, and at once asked President Wilson to "take in hand the restoration of peace", using his Fourteen Points as the basis for negotiations. Ludendorff was replaced by General Wilhelm Groener: although the German army still fought on in the west – a formidable instrument even in defeat – the Flanders coast had now fallen, the British were approaching Tournai and Valenciennes, and the Americans were all but through the Argonne.

Then, on October 24 the Italians began their final offensive against the tottering Austrians. The Emperor Karl warned Kaiser Wilhelm that he would seek an immediate armistice and pursue a separate peace. The German High Seas Fleet began to mutiny, and Kiel was in the hands of mutineers by November 4. The Kaiser left Berlin for the army's headquarters at Spa, where Groener bluntly told him that the army was no longer behind him: on November 9 he abdicated. Meanwhile, an armistice commission had crossed the lines on November 7. It met an Allied delegation led by Foch, and agreed an armistice which came into effect at 11 a.m. on November 11: the war was over.

TRENCH LIFE

Trench warfare was not especially lethal: troops were more vulnerable when they left their trenches to attack, or were driven from them by the enemy. It was at least moderately dangerous, with occasional shelling and sniping, although there were "quiet sectors" – like the Somme before the 1916 offensive – where "live and let live" prevailed. Yet even then troops were at the mercy of the elements, water and mud, and were the prey of rats and body lice. At night, when movement was safer, they would be busy repairing defences, and carrying up "trench stores" like sandbags, duckboards, iron pickets and wire.

BELOW

When field guns were not busy they were loaded and laid on a recorded target called the SOS. Troops could call down fire on the SOS by sending up coloured rockets in a prearranged sequence. These are in a trench in the Arleux sector held by 12th East Yorkshires, January 9, 1918.

ABOVE

Rats were common in the trenches, feeding on discarded food and unburied bodies, and becoming so bold that they would scramble over men sleeping in dug-outs. Men hunted them with firearms or cudgels, and, where possible, used dogs to catch them. This terrier served with the Middlesex Regiment on the Western Front.

Officers of 12th East Yorkshires washing and shaving in their dug-out, January 9, 1918. Dug-outs like this were usually cramped, damp and smelly. Their safety was relative: they survived hits by all but the heaviest guns, but an enemy who surprised a front-line trench would usually clear its dug-outs with hand grenades.

RIGHT

The commanding officer and officers of 12th Royal Irish Rifles wading through a communication trench, which had recently been taken over from the French, February 7, 1918. Trenches required constant repair, especially in frost and snow: one reason for the Fifth Army's poor showing on March 21 was the bad condition of many of its trenches.

THE LUDENDORFF OFFENSIVES: THE BRITISH VIEW

On March 21, 1918, the Germans launched an offensive with the aim of knocking Britain out of the war. They had 74 attacking divisions on a front of 80 kilometres (50 miles), supported by 6,608 guns and 3,534 mortars. The British Fifth Army, upon which the heaviest blow fell, had only 14 divisions to hold 45 kilometres (28 miles). The March offensive came close to taking the communication centre of Amiens, but ran out of steam within sight of it. Other offensives, in Flanders in April, on the Chemin des Dames in May, and further south in June and July, made impressive gains, but failed to capture key objectives or break Allied morale.

ABOVE

These British soldiers, killed on March 21, seem to have been victims of the bombardment whose suddenness, weight and precision were key ingredients of German success that day.

ABOVE
Stores and hutments are burnt to render
them valueless to the Germans while gun
teams go forward to recover their guns as
the retreat goes on. Omiecourt, March 24.

RIGHT
A 60-pdr battery in action in the open
near Albert, March 28, 1918. Albert, just
behind the British lines during the Battle
of the Somme in 1916, fell to the Germans
on March 26.

RIGHT
Old Bill in adversity: a soldier of the
Royal Irish, captured in March 1918.

OPPOSITE
"Georgette'" known to the British as the
Battle of the Lys, made substantial gains
in Flanders. These men of the Middlesex
Regiment hold a barricade in a Bailleul
street just before the town's fall, April 15.

BELOW
A train filled with walking wounded
stopping just outside Amiens, March 24.

ABOVE

Gas casualties of the 11th Brigade, Australian Imperial Force, lying out in the open at a crowded Casualty Clearing Station near Bois de l'Abbée, May 27.

RIGHT

Ludendorff's attacks were well supported by aircraft, some of them, in "battle squadrons", designated for ground attack. These machine gunners are engaging a hostile aircraft near Haverskerque on May 1, at the end of the Battle of the Lys.

LEFT

Alfresco headquarters: a runner (right) delivers a message to the officers of a reserve company of the Duke of Wellington's Regiment at Carvin, June 18, 1918.

BELOW

Many French and Belgian civilians left their homes in the path of German offensives. These refugees are on the road at Noeux-les-Mines, behind the 1915 Loos battlefield, on April 13.

THE LUDENDORFF OFFENSIVES: THE GERMAN VIEW

The Germans developed stormtroop units from 1915 onwards, and increased their numbers after Verdun. Their tactics emphasized the use of tough, self-reliant infantry, with their own machine guns, mortars, flame-throwers and light artillery, who sought gaps rather than surfaces, leaving serious opposition to mopping-up units following on behind. The artillery tactics perfected by Colonel Georg Bruchmüller provided them first with a sudden and savage preliminary bombardment and then with a creeping barrage whose pace they could affect with signal rockets. Stormtroops – "princes of the trenches" – represented a new warrior ideal, and the image of the loose-limbed fighter survived to mark German politics after the war.

Anglo-American authors are sometimes given to over-celebrating German military excellence. However, in both world wars the Germans often succeeded because of the attention they paid to doctrinal development and training. These stormtroops are training for the attack using dummy trenches at Sedan in 1917.

German reserves advancing up the
Albert–Bapaume road which crossed the
old Somme battlefield, March 1918.

The offensive gains momentum: German
cavalry crossing a captured British trench
near Ervillers, west of St Quentin. A British
Lewis gunner lies dead behind his weapon.

PREVIOUS PAGES
This photograph apparently shows
stormtroops mounting a genuine assault.
They moved fast, so as to take advantage
of the bombardment, and carried the bare
necessities required for combat, notably
weapons, water, ammunition and grenades.

ABOVE
A 77-mm field gun of an infantry
accompanying battery provides direct
support to attacking stormtroops. The layer
(second from left) can see the target he is
engaging, while the detachment commander
(left) observes the fire through binoculars.
Note the distinctive bayonet tassel worn
by the gunner nearest the camera: its
colours indicate the wearer's battery.

ABOVE
The Germans enjoyed an early lead in
trench-mortars, and throughout the war
their *minenwerfer* (literally mine-throwers)
were formidable. This 170-mm medium
minenwerfer could fire a 37-lb bomb
1,100 yards. Its wheels (right) enabled its
detachment to manhandle it with ropes and
handspikes, and were removed before firing.

The Germans captured well-stocked British dumps and gorged themselves on captured supplies. This produced serious difficulties, leading one German officer to maintain that the advance was not stopped by lack of German fighting spirit, but by an excess of captured Scottish drinking spirit.

The Germans lagged behind the Allies in tank development. The design for their A7V *Sturmpanzerwagen* was agreed in December 1916 and 100 tanks were ordered a year later, though fewer were produced. The A7V had a crew of eighteen and carried a captured Belgian 57-mm gun and six machine guns.

In theory Supreme War Lord but in practice figurehead: the Kaiser (left) and the Crown Prince of Prussia (right, with Hindenburg) at a party at army headquarters at Spa, held to celebrate the thirtieth anniversary of the Kaiser's accession, June 15.

German successes in the spring and early summer of 1918 left their army on the Western Front badly over-extended and vulnerable to counterattack. These prisoners, in a depot at Abbeville, were taken when the Hindenburg Line was broken in September.

The face of battle, 1918. Infantry of 1st Australian Division moving up near Harbonnières, east of Amiens, after a light "whippet" tank (background) had dealt with machine-gun posts that had held up the advance.

THE ALLIED COUNTEROFFENSIVE

The French launched a limited counterattack in July, and on August 8, Rawlinson, who replaced Gough in command of what was soon reconstituted as the Fourth Army, mounted a major attack east of Amiens, with Australian and Canadian troops playing lead roles. Ludendorff called it "the black day of the German army in the war." In late August Byng's Third Army on Rawlinson's left, attacked across the old Somme battlefield, and by early September the Allies were facing the Germans in the Hindenburg Line, their last major defensive position.

German prisoners taken at the Battle of Amiens. The battle began on August 8, and by its close on the 13th the British, and the French to their south, had killed or wounded 18,000 Germans and captured 30,000.

ABOVE
A 60-pdr in action in the open, August 10.
Life on a busy gun-line was dominated by
ammunition flow. Men at the limber (left)
are as busy as those on the gun: one gunner
is fusing shells, while another moves
forward with two-bag charges of cordite.

This all-purpose photograph of infantry and tanks has often been mis-captioned, not least by the author! In fact it shows the capture of Grevillers by the New Zealand Division, supported by tanks of 10th Battalion the Tank Corps on August 25. A clue to the troops' origin is the characteristic "lemon-squeezer" hat on a post, left front.

ABOVE

Although the German army showed
growing signs of indiscipline and weariness,
it never broke. These machine gunners have
manned their 1908/15 light machine gun
in a hastily dug shell-scrape to the last.

RIGHT

The original caption terms this "a sad but
necessary duty." A British soldier killed at
Chipilly on the Somme on August 10 is
searched for identification and personal
effects. The former will ensure that his
death is formally notified, by War Office
telegram and official letter, and his grave
properly marked: the latter will be sent to
his next of kin.

THE FINAL PUSH

In the last Hundred Days of the war the British army pushed across northwestern France, suffering some 300,000 casualties in the process, but taking about twice as many prisoners as the French, Americans and Belgians combined. It was a remarkable effort by an army consisting of 50 per cent 18-year-olds, which bore all the strains of a long and costly war. Perhaps it is a reflection of a British preoccupation with disasters that while the first day on the Somme and the muddy slog of Passchendaele are alike well remembered, the stunning achievement of the Hundred Days is too often ignored.

BELOW

As warfare became more fluid, so men found themselves living in extemporized defences rather than in formal trench systems. These British soldiers are washing and shaving in the hole made by a heavy shell on Mount Kemmel, south of Ypres, September 2.

LEFT
There were visible signs that German morale was crumbling: these Germans are surrendering to the advancing 45th Battalion Australian Imperial Force as it nears the Hindenburg Line, 18 September.

BELOW
A corporal of the Hampshire Regiment uses his compass to estimate the destination of propaganda leaflets. His assistant cuts a slit in the base of the balloon to allow gas to escape when it expands as the balloon rises. The leaflets are threaded on a slow fuse which will release them as it burns.

ABOVE

Horses pulling an 18-pdr up the slope of the
cutting of the Canal du Nord at Moeuvres,
near Cambrai, September 27. British gun
teams were reduced from six to four horses
to supply horses to the Americans.

ABOVE
Mark V tanks of 8th Battalion, Tank Corps, attached to 5th Australian Division for its crossing of the Hindenburg Line at Bellicourt, where the St Quentin Canal, which had been incorporated into the line, passed through a long tunnel, September 29. The tanks carry "cribs", which were dropped into trenches to help them cross.

PREVIOUS PAGES
**The victorious British XI Corps'
entry into Lille, October 18.**

ABOVE
The shape of things to come. Winston Churchill,
Minister of Munitions, (centre foreground) at
the parade celebrating the liberation of Lille.
The Second World War commander of Eighth
Army, then temporary Lieutenant Colonel
Bernard Montgomery, Chief of Staff of 47th
London Division, stands in the left foreground.

THE ALLIES UNDER PRESSURE

British success in 1918 owed much to the Herculean efforts of the French army over the previous years. Pétain, its commander in chief, was profoundly cautious, and believed that the Allies should stand on the defensive and await the arrival of the Americans. When the Germans attacked in March 1918 he feared that they would break the British, and planned to swing back to cover Paris if the Germans seemed likely to split the Allied armies. However, the Alliance held firm, and Foch's appointment as Allied commander in chief made it easier to switch troops to meet specific threats.

ABOVE
British wounded passing through the Franco-British outpost line, with a Hotchkiss machine gun in a hastily dug trench, at Roye, south of the Somme, on March 25.

RIGHT
Portugal had sent an expeditionary force to France in 1917, and it went into the line near Neuve Chapelle, where it was sharply attacked on April 9, 1918 at the start of the Battle of the Lys. These Portuguese troops – whose blue-grey uniforms led to them being mistaken for Serbs – are taking rations forward near Merville, April 12.

ABOVE

Foch sent reinforcements northwards to
help the British during the Battle of the Lys.
These French soldiers are advancing through
Caestre, near Hazebrouck, on April 13, as a
British 6-inch howitzer is being towed back.

RIGHT

In December 1915 General Jean-Baptiste
Estienne, father of the French tank arm,
gained permission to experiment with the
tank that became the Renault FT, shown
here returning from an attack on the
Aisne front. The first were used in March
1918, and there were 2,720 in service on
November 11.

OVER THERE

America's entry into the war had a profound effect, raising Allied morale and provoking Ludendorff into making his gambler's throws between March and July 1918. Almost two million Americans were eventually shipped to France, and as many again enlisted but never left the United States. Although America's combat contribution was relatively small – around 400,000 were actually engaged in the Meuse–Argonne offensive in October and November – John Maynard Keynes was right to observe that "without the assistance of the United States the Allies could never have won the War."

BELOW
American troops landing at Le Havre, July 12, 1918. Their build and bearing aroused much comment: one senior British officer told an American general that they were "the best types of men (physically and mentally) that they had ever seen."

What were then called "coloured troops" practice bayonet fighting at Gondrecourt, August 13. The US Army was segregated, and most black soldiers were posted to the Service of Supply. Only two black combat divisions went to France: the 92nd served alongside white American divisions, while the four regiments of the 93rd were sent to four French divisions.

The US army's rapid expansion outstripped the ability of domestic industry to supply it, and much weapons and equipment were provided by the British and French. This Renault FT tank, driver's and gunner's hatches open and turret traversed, was photographed at the Tank Corps school near Langres on July 15.

RIGHT
American machine-gunners in action near Villers Tournelle, May 20, 1918. The strips of ammunition are for the French-supplied Hotchkiss machine gun.

LEFT
Captain Eddie Rickenbacker with his Spad 13. The leading US ace, eventually credited with 24.33 victories (shared victories were fictionalized), Rickenbacker was a prewar racing driver, who went to France as a chauffeur and made his first operational flight in March 1918. He served again in the Second World War, surviving 22 days on a raft in the Pacific.

RIGHT
US infantry in the line near Bazoches, between the Vesle and the Aisne, September 4. Pershing was adamant that the AEF would fight as an American army, not split up amongst the Allies, but he was prepared to allow some of his divisions to support the British and French, and part of the US II Corps fought under British command until the war's end.

ABOVE

During September 12–16 the AEF, with
French support, pinched out a substantial
German salient at St-Mihiel, south of
Verdun. Although the operation demonstrated American inexperience, it was a
notable propaganda coup, reinforced here
by changing the name of a street in a
captured village from Hindenburgstrasse
to Wilson USA.

ABOVE

A French-supplied 340-mm gun, manned by men of the US Coast Artillery, in action at Baleycourt behind the Meuse–Argonne front, late September.

RIGHT

Although there were frequent complaints about poor food and accommodation, desertion was comparatively rare. Twenty-four American deserters were sentenced to death between April 1917 and November 1918, and none was actually shot. Here, a straggler and a deserter are publicly humiliated at Florient, 5 November.

The entrance to the canal with the mole in the background. HMS *Thetis* was sunk outside the canal entrance, but HMS *Iphegenia* and HMS *Intrepid* were sunk diagonally across the fairway: their crews were taken off by launch.

ZEEBRUGGE

On St George's Day (April 23) 1918 the British attacked Ostend and Zeebrugge in an effort to prevent German submarines and destroyers from using them. At Zeebrugge, where the main effort was made, the canal entrance was protected by a large and well-defended mole, connected to land by a railway viaduct. The mole was attacked by the cruiser HMS *Vindictive*, which was badly damaged before getting alongside to land her marines. An old submarine filled with explosive destroyed the viaduct, and three block-ships were sunk in the canal. Submarines were, however, still able to use it.

Members of *Vindictive*'s crew after their return. Five VCs were won when she attacked the mole under very heavy fire. On May 9–10 *Vindictive* was used as a blockship at Ostend.

THE ITALIAN FRONT

Although their German support had been withdrawn to the Western Front, in June the Austrians mounted an offensive. Conrad von Hötzendorf (now commanding Eleventh Army) attacked in the Trentino and Boroevic on the Piave, but it was only on the Piave that there was a glimmer of success. The Italians, commanded by the level-headed Armando Diaz, who had succeeded Cadorna in November 1917, followed up cautiously. On October 24, the anniversary of Caporetto, Diaz mounted his last offensive. The Battle of Vittorio Veneto began disappointingly for the Italians, but the exhausted Austrians were comprehensively defeated, asking for an armistice on November 3.

BELOW

Italian troops on the march in the Val d'Assa. Italy entered the war poorly prepared in terms or morale and social cohesion, and her code of military discipline was draconian: about 750 men were shot after Caporetto. But by 1918 morale had improved, reflecting a genuine sense of national commitment to the war.

ABOVE

In November 1917 the British sent Plumer, the most reliable of their army commanders, to Italy with substantial reinforcements, and three British divisions remained on the Italian front till the end of the war. This heavy gun is shown in action on December 31, 1917.

BELOW

Highlanders bringing Austrian prisoners over the Piave, November 22, 1918.

ABOVE
The Austrian army finally collapsed at
Vittorio Veneto with the loss of over half
a million prisoners.

RUSSIA IN 1918

Peace negotiations began at Brest-Litovsk in December 1917 and were concluded in March 1918. Trotsky, head of the Russian delegation, was a skilful negotiator, and on February 10 he refused to sign harsh German terms and proclaimed a state of "neither peace nor war" and the demobilization of the Russian army. This simply induced the Germans to move eastwards, capturing more territory and equipment, and prevailing on Lenin to instruct Trotsky to sign. Russia lost her Baltic provinces, Finland and the Caucasus, and the Germans would remain in occupation till the conclusion of a general peace.

BELOW
German foreign minister Kuhlmann signs the peace treaty at Brest-Litovsk on March 3, with Czernin, his Austrian counterpart, behind him.

LEFT
Leon Trotsky, who had played a major role in the October Revolution, headed the Russian delegation at Brest-Litovsk, where his skill and passion were no counterweight to Russia's impossible military situation.

BELOW
Tsar Nicholas II had abdicated in 1917, and was shot with his family in this house in Ekaterinburg in 1918.

THE END IN MESOPOTAMIA

In 1917 British-Indian forces in Mesopotamia had taken Baghdad and then sent columns up the Tigris, Euphrates and Diyala rivers. In 1918 Lieutenant General Sir William Marshall, who had taken command when Maude died of cholera, sent a small force under Major General L. C. Dunsterville to the Caspian. Marshall defeated the Turks at Mosul, and went on to occupy the town. His army by then numbered half a million men and had the biggest river fleet in the world, with 1,824 vessels.

BELOW

Jat soldiers of the Indian army's 113th Infantry firing rifle grenades. A metal spigot attached to the grenade was slipped into the rifle muzzle, and a ballestite cartridge then blew it on its way.

ABOVE

Turks surrendering to a British
outpost near Kirkuk, May 1918.

BELOW

A Squadron of 13th Hussars fording the
Hasa Su at Kirkuk, May 8, 1918.
Horsemen played a distinguished part in
the campaign. "Not even in Palestine,"
writes the Marquess of Anglesey, the
British cavalry's historian, "did the
cavalry attain to greater efficiency."

PALESTINE

Allenby captured Jerusalem late in 1917, but was ordered to send troops to France after the German offensive of March 1918. This left him too weak to attack as planned, but in the meantime the Arabs cut the Hejaz railway and isolated the Turkish garrison of Medina. Allenby's opponent, Liman von Sanders, who had taken over from Falkenhayn in March, was in growing difficulties, for the Turkish government diverted reinforcements to the Caucasus. On September 19 Allenby broke the Turkish line on the coast and then exploited north and east in a battle aptly called Megiddo, the modern version of the biblical Armageddon. An armistice was concluded at Mudros on October 30.

ABOVE
Men of 2/14th London Regiment (The London Scottish) marching through Es Salt after its capture, April 2, 1918.

LEFT
Fakri Pasha, described by Lawrence as a "courageous old butcher", commander of XII Corps, surrenders to the Emir Abdullah at Bir Derwish. The Arabs hovered on Allenby's right flank, cutting the Hejaz railway and diverting Turkish resources from the Palestine front. In January 1918 they seized Tafila, their most famous victory over regular troops.

ABOVE
Turkish prisoners taken during the Battle of Megiddo, September 24. The commander of the Turkish 16th Division is seated on the right, wearing a white arm-band. In the centre some prisoners are receiving rations, while others move off to form a column for the march to prison camps.

RIGHT
Damascus fell on October 1. These members of the Australian Light Horse, bivouacked outside the city, had played an important role in a campaign where dash and mobility were invaluable.

THE WAR IN THE AIR

In 1918 the war in the air, like that on the ground, see-sawed back and forth. The German March offensive was supported by abundant air power, with many aircraft assigned specifically to the strafing of troops on the ground. But by August the Allies had the edge, and the attack at Amiens was supported by 1,000 aircraft, 800 of them British, from the newly formed Royal Air Force. Aircraft spotted for the guns, kept German patrols at bay, strafed, and even dropped machine-gun ammunition to advancing units.

BELOW

A British airfield on the Western Front, 1918. The zig-zag lines of trenches stand out clearly, but the absence of wire suggests that these are not part of a front-line system but defences in depth, probably dug as a result of German successes in the spring.

ABOVE

The pilot and observer of an RE8 reconnaissance aircraft of No 59 Squadron RAF receive
last minute instructions from Major C. J.
Mackay MC, their squadron commander,
May 15. The RE8 – nicknamed "Harry Tate",
in rhyming slang, after a popular music hall
comedian, was the most widely used British
two-seater. Note the observer's machine gun
mounted on a Scarff ring.

RIGHT

Freiherr Manfred von Richthofen, the "Red
Baron" was a regular cavalry officer who
learnt to fly in 1916 and commanded
Jagdgeschwader I (the "Flying Circus")
composed of several squadrons. Germany's
top-scoring air ace, with 80 kills, he was
shot down in 1918, probably by Australian
machine-gun fire.

ABOVE

The crew of an Armstrong-Whitworth FK8 (a two-seater light bomber and reconnaissance aircraft) shot down near Mericourt. Aircraft often caught fire when hit, giving airmen the ghastly choice of burning, or jumping to a certain death. These two chose to stay with their burning plane.

LEFT

A member of the Chinese Labour Corps on an airfield in France. China joined the Allies in August 1917, but prior to that large numbers of Chinese served on contract with Allied forces, often as labourers but also in more skilled trades. There were nearly 100,000 with the British army on the Western Front in 1918, about as many with the French and 5,000 with the Americans.

ARMISTICE

It took time for the Supreme War Council to agree to outline terms, but on November 5 the Germans were informed that they could apply for an armistice. The German delegation crossed the lines on the evening of the 7th, and was taken to Rethondes in the Forest of Compiègne, where discussions took place in Foch's railway carriage. The Germans obtained a few slight concessions before signing an armistice which came into effect at 11 a.m. on November 11. Matthias Erzberger, head of their delegation, concluded with the prophetic words: "A nation of seventy millions suffers but does not die."

Foch (second from right) stands outside the railway carriage after signing the armistice. Other signatures on the photograph are those of Admiral Sir Rosslyn Wemyss, First Sea Lord, and General Maxime Weygand, Foch's chief of staff. Weygand was recalled to command the French army in 1940, a month before the armistice between France and Germany was signed in precisely the same place.

PREVIOUS PAGES
Celebrations outside Buckingham
Palace in London on November 11.

ABOVE
Two officers of the Irish Guards read
armistice news to their men, November 12.
The photograph was taken at Maubeuge,
where the BEF had concentrated in August
1914: the last British soldier to die in the
war fell at Mons, where the British army
had fired its first shots.

LEFT

The ex-Kaiser crossing the Dutch frontier on November 9, the day of his abdication. Although there was talk of arraigning him for war crimes – there was a "Hang the Kaiser" lobby in Britain – he lived his life out undisturbed at his estate at Doorn. He died in 1941, when Holland was under German occupation.

BELOW

Retrospect and portent. On December 8 a parade on the esplanade of Metz, surrendered in 1870 but now French once more, saw Pétain awarded his marshal's baton. Behind him stand (left to right) Joffre, Foch, Haig (with the dapper Weygand visible behind him) Pershing, Gillain (Belgium) Albricci (Italy) and Heller (Poland).

AFTERMATH

THE ARMISTICE CONCLUDED near Compiègne on November 11 was just that: a cessation of hostilities, like those that had already been agreed with the Austrians and Italians, not a peace treaty. Early in 1919 delegates met in Paris to work on the replacement of regional armistices by a permanent general peace; this was to become the Treaty of Versailles. There was little unanimity among the wartime Allies. Clemenceau, the French premier, hoped to see Germany permanently weakened, while Lloyd George, the British prime minister, was personally more conciliatory but knew that the British public expected a stern peace. President Wilson's Fourteen Points had been very influential in 1918, but they were not based on a deep understanding of European politics, and Wilson's own position grew weaker when his Democrats lost the Congressional elections that year. The Italians sought to see the secret agreements which had brought them into the war honoured. Some other belligerents had entered the war late precisely in the hope of having a seat at the conference, and many national groups who hoped to become states had sent delegations. Neither the vanquished nor neutrals were present, and the Russians, engaged in an increasingly bitter civil war, were also unrepresented.

The main Treaty of Versailles deprived Germany of Alsace and Lorraine, which were returned to France, and two small areas that were ceded to Belgium. The Saar basis, abutting Lorraine, was to be administered by the newly constituted League of Nations: France was to own its coal mines for fifteen years, at the conclusion of which a plebiscite would determine whether the region would be returned to Germany or annexed by France. The Rhineland was to be demilitarized. Large areas of eastern territory were given to the re-established state of Poland. This left the German city of Danzig marooned in Polish territory, and East Prussia separated from the rest of Germany. Danzig was accordingly made a free state under the supervision of the League of Nations, and the Germans were given access to East Prussia across the "Polish corridor". All Germany's colonies were handed to the League for disposal. The German army was to be limited to 100,000 men, and there were sharp restrictions on the equipment the Germans could possess: they could have no tanks, no aircraft and no submarines. Finally, Germany was to accept a clause admitting guilt for causing the war, and was to pay reparations for damage inflicted during it. The latter, notified to Germany by the Reparations Commission in 1921, amounted to an enormous 33 billion dollars, repayment of which was to be spread over thirty years – to be paid by a state with an unfavourable balance of trade and which had been deprived of some of its richest industrial areas.

The Austro-Hungarian Empire was dismembered by the treaties of St Germain-en-Laye and Trianon. Austria and Hungary were split. Bohemia, Moravia and much of Austrian Silesia went to the new state of Czechoslovakia, Galicia went to Poland, and Teschen was divided between Poland and Czechoslovakia. The Bukovina was ceded to Romania. Italy took the Trentino, Trieste, Istria and some Dalmatian islands, as well as the German-speaking South Tyrol. Bosnia-Herzegovina and the Dalmatian coast joined Serbia in the new Kingdom of Serbs, Croats and Slovenes, later renamed Yugoslavia. The Austrian army was restricted to 30,000 men, and *anschluss* – union with Germany – was specifically forbidden. Hungary ceded Transylvania and much of the Banat to Romania, other territories to Yugoslavia, and a sliver of borderland to Austria. The Hungarian army was to be reduced to 35,000 men. The Treaty of Neuilly deprived Bulgaria of Western Thrace which went to Greece, and of some small border areas, ceded to Yugoslavia. The Treaty of Sèvres acknowledged what was already an accomplished fact, the destruction of the Turkish empire, but the nationalist outburst the treaty provoked saw the fall of the Turkish monarchy and compelled the negotiation of a new treaty.

Despite the objection that it was indeed a *diktat*, imposed upon the vanquished, and the fact that the new states it created embodied aggravated nationalism (often uneasily coupled with national minorities) and lacked natural borders, the Versailles settlement might not have proved so short-lived had America, chief among its midwives, not abandoned the infant immediately afterwards. The Senate did not ratify the treaty, and America not only elected a Republican president in 1920 but demobilized rapidly and made it clear that she had no further interest in European security. There were those who feared that the settlement would not last: Foch maintained that it was simply "an armistice for twenty years." The magnitude of destruction demanded international co-operation; the conflict had both inflamed national passions and left a deep residue of bitterness; the League of Nations lacked the ability to enforce its decisions; and the success of communism in Russia inspired fears that similar revolution would spread elsewhere.

The First World War was, as Hew Strachan has so brilliantly termed it, "one of the most unassailable divisions in the compartmentalization of the past." It levelled the proud tower that had glinted in the early summer of 1914, and its human losses – at the very least 15 million – resulted in a marked deficit of men after 1918. It was not simply that the loss was quantitative, but that so many of those who had been killed or crippled were those who might have provided leadership and stability in the 1920s and 1930s. Contemporaries were divided in their views on the impact of the war on the legitimacy of violence. For some it proved that war was no longer a legitimate instrument of state policy, and that pacifism was the individual's only correct moral stance. But for others it enshrined the principle that violence was, as a Spanish philosopher was to put it in 1932, "the means resorted to by him who had previously exhausted all others in the defence of the rights of justice which he thought he possessed." British soldiers had been encouraged to believe that they were fighting "the war to end war." Yet in its aftermath it became increasingly clear that war had not been abolished as a social institution, and that the good intentions of the Versailles peacemakers were to prove as transitory as the courage of those who had borne the brunt of what was all too undeniably the Great War.

GERMANY

In Germany, the unrest which had preceded the end of war did
not end with the armistice. The abdication of the Kaiser was
followed by the proclamation of a republic, but the new regime,
which was to take its name from its seat at Weimar, did not find it
easy to become established. In 1919 there was an uprising by the
Spartacists on the extreme left and by communists in Bavaria, and
in 1920 an attempted coup by members of the right-wing
Nationalist party. However, despite resentment at the harshness
of the Versailles settlement, and the growing legend that Germany
had been "stabbed in the back" from the home front, the Weimar
republic enjoyed support from a broad political centre.

BELOW
Soldiers of the 150th Infantry Regiment
returning to Berlin. Scenes like this helped
lay the foundation of the myth that this was
an army defeated by domestic politicians
not foreign enemies. German soldiers went
home remarkably quickly, and most did
their best to return to a normal life.

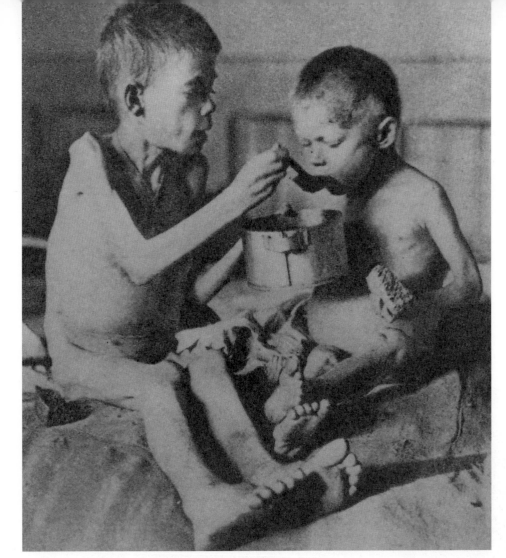

LEFT
The Allied blockade produced very real suffering in the Central Powers, and it was not substantially relaxed until the Versailles settlement was concluded. Scenes like this contributed to lasting resentment towards the peace and shocked Allied soldiers who saw them.

BELOW
Armed revolutionaries of the Spartacist movement in a Berlin street. The Spartacists were suppressed with the aid of *Freikorps*, which was composed of ex-soldiers. The Spartacist leaders, Rosa Luxemburg and Karl Liebknecht, were shot after their capture in 1919.

ABOVE

The Allies provided an Army of Occupation
that held strategically important areas of
western Germany and helped put pressure on
the German government to sign the treaty of
Versailles. Here, 1st Battalion The Grenadier
Guards crosses the Hohenzollern Bridge in
Cologne on January 8, 1919. Some 200,000
soldiers were in the British Army of the
Rhine, which was not withdrawn until 1929.

THE VERSAILLES SETTLEMENT

There was not a single treaty at Versailles. The main treaty with Germany took its name from Versailles itself, while others, in which the Allies made peace with the remaining defeated enemies, were named for the Trianon, part of the palace complex, and other nearby châteaux.

RIGHT

The Council of Four, the major Allied leaders at Versailles. Left to right: Orlando (Italy), Lloyd George (Great Britain) Clemenceau (France) and Wilson (USA). These politicians brought sharply different expectations with them to the conference table.

BELOW

The signing of the Treaty of Versailles in the Hall of Mirrors, June 28, 1919. This was the same room in which the German Empire had been proclaimed in January 1871.

THE HIGH SEAS FLEET

One of the conditions of the armistice was the surrender of
Germany's High Seas Fleet. Most German vessels sailed to
Scapa Flow in the Orkneys on November 21, 1918 and that
night were ordered to lower their German ensigns for the last
time. Given the importance of naval rivalry in the run-up to
the war, the act was deeply symbolic. However, the Germans
riposted with symbolism of their own, opening the sea-cocks
of their vessels to scuttle them on June 21, 1919.

ABOVE
This photograph taken from an airship
shows battleships of the High Seas Fleet
keeping good station on their way to
surrender at Scapa Flow, November 21.

RIGHT
The new battle cruiser, *Hindenburg* lies
scuttled at Scapa Flow, June 21, 1919.

ALLIED INTERVENTION IN RUSSIA

Civil War in Russia, between the communist Reds and the pro-Tsarist Whites, was complicated by the intervention of Allied contingents in support of the Whites. Some operated in the north, through the ports of Archangel and Murmansk, while others landed in the Crimea or eastern Russia. But while some Allied politicians advocated giving systematic large-scale support to the Whites – Churchill argued that Bolshevism should be "strangled at birth" – it was increasingly clear that their populations would not tolerate sustained military involvement in Russia, and troops were withdrawn in 1920.

LEFT

The Czech Legion, around 50,000 strong, originated from Czechs in the Tsarist army; many had been conscripts in the Austro-Hungarian army and had either deserted or been taken prisoner by the Russians. The Legion had begun to cross Siberia for Vladivostok when friction with the Bolsheviks led to its siding with the Whites: it secured many stations on the Trans-Siberian railway. This is a heavily armed, and camouflaged Czech armoured train.

BELOW

Atrocities were commonplace in the Russian Civil War, and Allied troops sometimes became involved, with captured soldiers, and especially their officers, being murdered out of hand. These British naval and military prisoners of war, photographed in Moscow, have been more fortunate.

VICTORY AND REMEMBRANCE

In the immediate aftermath of the war the victors celebrated their achievement and, like their former opponents, took steps to ensure that the sacrifices made by those who had died in the war should not be forgotten. In 1919 formal victory parades followed the popular rejoicing of 1918. The commemoration of the war went on with the erection of war memorials, in a wide variety of scales and styles, everywhere from capital cities to small villages.

BELOW

The French victory parade passes through the Arc de Triomphe on July 14, 1919. The size and splendour of this spectacle could not conceal the fact that France had lost 1.3 million dead, 27 per cent of all men between the ages of 18 and 27. France's demand for harshness at Versailles and her behaviour in 1940 are comprehensible only in the context of this loss.

LEFT

In 1920 both Britain and France decided to bury an unidentified corpse, chosen blindly from unidentified dead taken from several sectors, with full military honours. Here Britain's Unknown Warrior – the term deliberately chosen to imply inclusiveness of all the armed forces – rests at Boulogne, with a French guard of honour, prior to being taken to England.

BELOW

The Cenotaph (a symbolic empty tomb) in London's Whitehall, immediately prior to its unveiling by George V on November 11, 1920, the day of the Unknown Warrior's funeral in Westminster Abbey.

ABOVE
Members of the Women's Auxiliary Army Corps
tending graves at Abbeville, February 9, 1918.
The Imperial (now Commonwealth) War Graves
Commission was set up in 1917 to maintain
graves and build and maintain memorials to
those who have no known graves. Wooden
crosses like these were replaced with over
587,000 headstones by 1938.

Mussolini (centre) with First World War veterans and his fascist Blackshirts during the "March on Rome" of October 1922. Traditional political parties, weakened by dissension and discredited by corruption and incompetence, could not prevent his being summoned to head a plenipotentiary government. The bearded Emilio de Bono (third from left) helped vote Mussolini from power in 1943 and was shot for treason, while Dino Grandi (front row, right) moved the vote but avoided execution.

A BEGINNING IN AN END

Resentment at the Versailles settlement was not confined to the vanquished. Some German politicians argued that their soldiers had been let down by politicians in 1918, and that the settlement betrayed the understanding that peace would be concluded on the basis of Wilson's Fourteen Points. Hyperinflation sharply undermined cohesion and consensus, and the Wall Street Crash of 1929 accelerated the drift to extremism. Italy was disillusioned with the poor reward given her by the settlement, and by the slow economic recovery that followed it: many of her middle classes, fearing bolshevism, turned to Benito Mussolini's fascism.

Adolf Hitler addressing an early meeting of the National Socialist German Workers' Party at Munich in 1922. The following year he attempted a Mussolini-style coup in Munich and was imprisoned after its failure. He stood unsuccessfully against Hindenburg in the 1932 presidential elections, but was appointed chancellor in 1933 and swiftly began tearing up the provisions of the Versailles settlement.

INDEX

ACKNOWLEDGEMENTS

All the photographs reproduced in the book have been taken from the collections of the Photograph Archive at the Imperial War Museum. The Museum's reference numbers for each of the photographs are listed below, giving the page on which they appear in the book and any location indicator (t-top, b-bottom, l-left, r-right, c-centre)

10	Q106468	23b	Q22084	61	Q52827	105b	Q13392
12	Q81813	23b	Q22084	61	Q22492	106b	Q70704
13	HU50506	23t	Q38712	62	HU67825	106t	Q62973
13	Q81794	24	HU57550	63	Q85204	107	Q53874
14	Q81813	28b	Q91840	64	HU57678	108	Q114805
14	Q81822	28t	Q81831	65	Q53538	109b	Q115093
14	Q81788	29	Q81808	66	Q53537	109t	HU62455
15	Q81794	30	Q57096	67b	HU71985	110–11	Q53762
15	HU50506	31	Q65860	67t	Q53625	112	Q53768
15b	Q81834	32	Q81765	68b	Q53398	112b	HU68589
15t	Q81756	33	BQ81832	68t	Q53486	113	Q653763
16	Q81822	33t	Q81723	69	Q53517	114	Q53589
16	HU55928	34	Q67397	70	Q423033	115b	Q108330
16	Q81788	35	Q22325	71b	Q30071	115t	Q32930
17	Q81834	36	HU87473	71t	Q30067	116	HU52451
17	Q81756	36	HU63599	72–3	Q53286	117b	Q106215
17	Q114293	37b	Q38000	74	Q69146	117t	Q106217
18	Q114293	37t	Q57065	75	Q43476	118b	HU63277b
18	HU55928	38b	Q104370	76	HU57923	118t	Q49236
18b	Q82944	38t	Q97534	77	Q53359	119	Q60741
18t	Q91838	39	Q50992	78	Q50720	120	Q67644
19	Q91838	40	Q20896	79	HU35801	121b	Q90475
19	Q82944	41	Q22178	80	Q7071	121t	Q67656
19b	Q100052	42b	HU57680	84	Q48966	122b	Q49305
19t	Q100308	42t	Q55512	85	T Q51572	122t	HU51083
20	Q106468	43b	Q70071	86	HU35815	123	Q49296
20b	Q106468	43t	Q70070	87	Q49217	124	Q51067
20m	Q100052	44	Q51480	88	Q114867	125b	Q53596
20T	Q100308	45	Q51224	88b	Q48951	125t	Q53851
21B	HU53858	46b	Q53337	89	Q51647	126	Q53879
21b	HU53858	46t	Q51484	90	Q49751	127	Q42436
21t	HU53847	47	Q51486	91	Q49750	128	Q56992
21t	HU53847	48	HU71178	92b	Q22687	129b	HU69642
22b	HU17777	49b	Q81728	92t	HU36434	129t	Q32702
22b	HU1777	49t	Q100136	93	Q110494	130	Q4530
22t	HU68382	50	HU52449	94	Q53630	131b	Q81852
22t	HU68382	51b	Q52794	95b	Q78062	134b	Q510
		51t	THU57551	95t	Q107445	134t	Q3255
		52b	Q53523	96–7	Q58481	135b	HU57402
		52t	HU57550	96l	HU64169	135t	HU57661
		53	Q27170	98	Q93351	136b	Q106227
		54	Q70235	99b	HU59006	136C	Q34370
		55b	Q51506	99t	Q13547	136t	Q34370
		55t	Q109609	100b	SP452	137b	Q58026
		56b	Q60737	100m	SP682A	137t	Q106227
		56t	HU71992	100t	Q13783	138/9	Q460
		57b	Q57380	101	Q50473	140b	Q60465
		57t	Q56210	102b	Q69514	140t	Q56139
		58	HU35798	102t	A1090/Q112876	141bl	Q97325
		58b	Q57287	103	Q7071	141br	Q68200
		59	Q53230	104	HU50622	141t	Q98271
		60	Q14782	105	HU50621	142	Q27226

ACKNOWLEDGEMENTS

143b	Q90448	181b	HU63120	226	Q6354	272	Q72619
143t	HU55527	181t	HU57593	227	Q6311	273b	Q11322
144b	Q99767	182	E(AUS)3338	228b	Q67821	273t	E(Aus)3274
144t	Q78065	183br	Q98437	228t	Q15681	274	Q9347
145b	HU66822	183cl	Q54534	229b	SP986	275	Q9365
145t	Q69585	183t	Q97838	229t	Q15457	276–77	Q95579
146	Q23760	184	Q65158	230	Q67818	278	Q11428
147b	Q70068	185	Q65122	231	Q115126	279b	Q362
147t	Q78038	186b	Q65091	232	Q45338	279t	Q10824
148b	Q70437	186t	Q65097	233	Q86080	280b	Q56440
148t	Q4530	187	Q23855	234	Q24659	280t	Q8719
149	Q69481	188	HU72105	235b	Q24168	281	Q6850
150	Q73413	189	Q69958	235t	Q25222	282b	Hu70258
151b	Q101353	190	Q5095	236	MU64303	282t	Hu70259
151t	Q78086	194	Q20343	237b	Q50573	283b	Q70707
152b	Q41740	195b	SP2054	237m	Q59193	283m	Q114172
152t	Q78070	195t	Q45319	237tl	Q114044	283t	Q69949
153b	Q18593	196	Q19954	238b	Q13213b	284	Wy56409
153t	Q55499	196t	SP2073	238t	Q12937	285b	Q70742
154	Q82238	197	Q5095	239b	Q32826	285t	Q69946
155b	HU58254	198b	Q6412	239t	Q32740	286b	Wy46120
155C	SP1708	198t	Q5723	240b	Q98404	286t	Q49164
155t	HU69073	199	C01146	240t	Q60340	287	Q25946
156b	SP2470	200	Q56154	241b	Q52230	288b	Q26693
156c	SP2468	201b	Q53979	241t	HU66715	288t	Q26514
156t	Q20889	201t	Q5659	242-43	Q81095	289	Q652069
157b	Q20665	202b	Q70887	244b	Q79586	290	Q45331
157t	Q270257	202t	Q112247	244t	Q81094	291b	Q81132
158	Q42252	203	Q53994	245	Q103662	291t	Q23903
159	Q1375	204b	Q100257	246	Q106252	292	Q24791
160b	SP989	204t	Q70210	247b	Q69406	293b	Q24707
160t	HU64215	205	Q1787	247t	Q69411	293t	Q24662
161b	Q69876	206	Q1871	252b	Q10616	294	Q65465
161t	Q32203	207b	Q106079	252t	Q115420	295b	Q12355
162	Q718	207t	Q11853	253b	Q10682	295m	Q12977
163	Q36	208b	Q65535	253t	Q10623	295t	Q60001
164b	Q53	208m	Q68557	254	Q42245	296	Q93087
164t	Q754	208t	HU63634	255b	Q8647	297b	Q58028
165	Q79496	209	Q48212	255t	Q10797	297t	Q12168
166	Q4066	210	Q106271	256b	Q10795	298b	Q91411
167b	Q4057	211	Q30040	256t	Q23839	298t	Q58049
167t	Q7233	212b	Q19653	257	Q6530	299	Q43225
168b	Q3996	212t	Q108192	258b	Q6588	300/301	Q47894
168t	C0202	213b	Q109996	258t	E(Aus)4852	302	Q3365
169	Q3990	213t	Q109838	259b	Q10898	303b	Q46480
170–1	Q5817	214b	Q88190	259t	Q6714	303t	Q47933
172b	Q1142	214t	Q106565	260	Q55016	306	Q110891
172t	Q4079	215	E(AUS)632	261b	Q29889	307b	Q110864
173	Q872	216	Q2295	261t	Q57466	307t	Wu87721
173	Q872	217b	Q2293	262–63	Q47997	308	Q3492
174b	Q55482	217t	Q5460	264	Q56487	309b	Q14996
174t	Q1244	218/2A	E(AUS)715	265	Q23754	309t	Q48222
175	Q1309	218L	Q5724	266b	Q23739	310b	SP1635
176	Q1211	220b	E(AUS)694	266m	Q37343	310t	Q20614
177	Q5574	220t	Q5966	266t	Q65139	311b	Q71271
178b	Q2981	221	Q6236	267	Q9358	311t	Q61671
178t	Q5798	222b	Q3013	268b	Q9178	312	Q81860
179b	HU51796	222t	C02252	268t	E(Aus)2878	313b	Q14965
179b	HU51796	223	E(AUS)1223	269	CO3007	313t	Q70592
179C	HU51795	224	Q30515	270	Q11262	314	Q8467
179t	HU51794	225b	Q6432	271b	Q23563	315b	NYP68037
180	Q11434	225t	Q94496	271t	Q7928	315t	Wy48179